The Mature Church

THE MATURE CHURCH
A Rhetorical-Critical Study of Ephesians 4:1–16

Copyright © 2013 Emmanuel D. Mbennah. All rights reserved. Except for brief quotations in critical publications or reviews, no part of this book may be reproduced in any manner without prior written permission from the publisher. Write: Permissions, Wipf and Stock Publishers, 199 W. 8th Ave., Suite 3, Eugene, OR 97401.

Wipf & Stock
An imprint of Wipf and Stock Publishers
199 W. 8th Ave., Suite 3
Eugene, OR 97401

www.wipfandstock.com

ISBN 13: 978-1-62032-546-9

Manufactured in the U.S.A.

This is book is based on a dissertation for the Ph.D. in the New Testament.

The Mature Church

A Rhetorical-Critical Study of Ephesians 4:1–16

Emmanuel D. Mbennah

ASSOCIATE PROFESSOR EXTRAORDINARY,
NORTH-WEST UNIVERSITY, POTCHEFSTROOM, SOUTH AFRICA

WIPF & STOCK · Eugene, Oregon

Contents

List of Figures / ix
Preface / xi

1 **INTRODUCTION** / 1

2 **RHETORICAL CRITICISM IN NEW TESTAMENT HERMENEUTICS** / 5

2.1 Introduction

2.2 New Testament Hermeneutics
  2.2.1 Necessity of New Testament Hermeneutics
  2.2.2 Hermeneutical Issues in New Testament Interpretation
  2.2.3 Hermeneutical Considerations with Regard to the Epistles
  2.2.4 Rhetorical Criticism and New Testament Studies
  2.2.5 Summary

2.3 Methods of New Testament Rhetorical Criticism: An Appraisal
  2.3.1 Kennedy's Method of Rhetorical Criticism
  2.3.2 Trible's Method of Rhetorical Criticism
  2.3.3 Cornelius' Method of Rhetorical Criticism

2.4 Towards a Method of Rhetorical Criticism for New Testament Interpretation
  2.4.1 A Theory of Rhetoric
  2.4.2 Rhetoric as Persuasion
  2.4.3 Rhetorical Dimensions of the First Readers
  2.4.4 Rhetorical Dimensions of the Text
  2.4.5 Rhetorical Dimensions of the Author
  2.5 Summary

Contents

3 **COMMUNICATIVE FUNCTION OF EPHESIANS 4:1–16 / 45**

3.1 Introduction

3.2 Rhetoricity of the Epistle to the Ephesians

    3.2.1 The Rhetorical Dimensions of the Author

    3.2.2 The Rhetorical Dimensions of the Recipients

    3.2.3 The Rhetorical Purpose in Ephesians

3.3 Rhetorical Structure of Ephesians

    3.3.1 Outline of Ephesians

    3.3.2 The New Identity of the Gentile Christians (Eph 1–3)

        3.3.2.1 Blessed Be God: Invitation to Celebrating God's Wonder

        3.3.2.2 New Identity of the Gentile Christians

        3.3.2.3 "Then" but "Now"

        3.3.2.4 God Included You in His Eternal Plan (3:1–13)

        3.3.2.5 Know This God and Be Filled with His Fullness (3:14–21)

    3.3.3 The Necessary Middle (4:1–16)

    3.3.4 Responsibility in the New Identity (4:17–6:20)

3.4 The Place of 4:1–16 in Ephesians

3.5 Summary

4 **THE MEANING AND IMPERATIVE OF CHRISTIAN SPIRITUAL MATURITY / 73**

4.1 Introduction

4.2 Thought Structure of 4:1–16

    4.2.1 The Thought Structure on a Micro Level

    4.2.2 4:13 in the Context of 4:1–16

    4.2.3 The Parallel Proposition of the Three Clauses

    4.2.4 The Sequence Proposition of the Three Clauses

    4.2.5 The Mixed Proposition of the Three Clauses

    4.2.6 An Alternative Proposition of the Three Clauses

4.3 Analysis and Interpretation of 4:13

    4.3.1 Until We All Attain

Contents

4.3.2 Unity of the Faith, and of the Knowledge of the Son of God

4.3.3 Unto a Perfect Man

4.3.4 Unto the Measure of the Stature of the Fullness of Christ

4.4 The Meaning of Christian Spiritual Maturity

4.5 The Imperative of Christian Spiritual Maturity

    4.5.1 Lack of Christian Spiritual Maturity Is Dangerous for Christians

    4.5.2 False Teachers, and Their False Teachings and Methods Are Difficult to Discern and Resist

4.6 Conclusion

5 SPIRITUAL MATURITY IN THE CHURCH: A CASE STUDY / 97

5.1 Introduction

5.2 Analysis of Data and Interpretation of Findings

5.3 Discussion

    5.3.1 Understanding of the Meaning and Essence of Spiritual Maturity

    5.3.2 Understanding of the Means to Spiritual Maturity

    5.3.3 Understanding of the Indicators of Spiritual Maturity

    5.3.4 Understanding of When or Whether Spiritual Maturity Will Be Complete

    5.3.5 Understanding of the Necessity of Spiritual Maturity

    5.3.6 Level of Spiritual Maturity of the Church Leadership

5.4 Understanding and Level of Spiritual Maturity of the Church Leaders

    5.4.1 The Meaning and Essence of Spiritual Maturity

    5.4.2 The Means to Spiritual Maturity

    5.4.3 The Indicators of Spiritual Maturity

    5.4.4 When or Whether Spiritual Maturity Will Be Complete

    5.4.5 The Necessity of Spiritual Maturity

    5.4.6 The Level of Spiritual Maturity of the Leadership

5.5 Summary

Contents

6 **SPIRITUAL MATURITY IN EPHESIANS 4:13–16 AND THE CHURCH: LESSONS FROM THE CASE STUDY / 125**

   6.1 Introduction

   6.2 Comparing Spiritual Maturity in Ephesians 4:13–16 and the Understanding of Spiritual Maturity of Church Leadership

   6.3 Evaluation of the Church Leaders' Understanding of Spiritual Maturity and Its Implications

      6.3.1 Meaning and Essence of Spiritual Maturity
      6.3.2 The Means to Attainment of Spiritual Maturity
      6.3.3 The Point of Attainment of Spiritual Maturity
      6.3.4 The Indicators of Progression towards Spiritual Maturity
      6.3.5 Specific Key Indicators of Spiritual Maturity
      6.3.6 The Necessity of Spiritual Maturity

   6.4 Evaluation of the Level of Spiritual Maturity and Its Implications

   6.5 Summary

7 **CONCLUSION / 141**

Bibliography / 149
Index / 157

List of Figures

The Thought Structure of 4:1–16 on a Micro Level / 76–78

Figure 5.1—Highest Educational Levels of the Respondents / 99

Figure 5.2— Respondent's Role in the Church / 100

Figure 5.3—Statement that Describes Spiritual Maturity Most Accurately according to the Respondents / 100

Figure 5.4—The Meaning of Spiritual Maturity according to the Respondents / 101

Figure 5.5—What Is to Be Done to People Who Teach Wrong Doctrines in the Church? / 101

Figure 5.6— How Spiritual Maturity Comes About according to the Respondents / 102

Preface

THE AIM OF THIS book is to determine and present the meaning of spiritual maturity in Ephesians 4:1–16 and demonstrate its use as a critical standard to evaluate the spiritual maturity of the church. To achieve this aim, a method of rhetorical criticism appropriate for interpreting Ephesians 4:1–16 is developed and, accordingly, the communicative function of Ephesians 4:1–16 in the epistle determined. Ephesians 4:13 is then interpreted to obtain the meaning of spiritual maturity. A self-administered questionnaire was developed, pre-tested, and distributed to a sample of church leaders in a specific context. The data from the questionnaires returned were analyz\ ed. The meaning of spiritual maturity in Ephesians 4:1–16 and the understanding and level of spiritual maturity of the leadership of the church were compared. The following are some of the highlights of the results and conclusions:

First, Paul's main purpose in Ephesians is for Christians to understand that they have a new identity and to exhort them to celebrate it (Eph 1–3). In response, they are to live a life that is commensurate with that identity as an expression of their gratitude to God for it (4:17—6:20); but in order to be able to live as exhorted, they need to be growing towards spiritual maturity (4:1–16).

Second, spiritual maturity is a final destination intended for all Christians, who are progressively becoming one body that befits Christ as its Head. Its indicators include stability and constancy in the truth, ability to discern error and reject or correct it, and ability and orientation to speak the truth in love. As a result of the church growing towards ultimate spiritual maturity, unity increasingly becomes a reality, implying that it is spiritual maturity that brings about unity, not the other way around.

Third, in several of the dimensions of spiritual maturity, the church leadership's understanding is not in agreement with Ephesians 4:1–16. That is by no means to say the church leadership does not agree with this portion of Scripture on anything. For example, in consonance with the position of Ephesians 4:13, the church leadership generally acknowledges the necessity of human effort to strive towards spiritual maturity and the necessity of systematic and authentic biblical teaching for the attainment of spiritual maturity. This is significant, since without such acknowledgement, investing towards spiritual maturity in terms of time, finances, and training is highly unlikely. However, whereas the corporate essence of spiritual maturity in Ephesians 4:13 projects an expectation of increasing oneness of the body, the church leadership understands the corporate essence of spiritual maturity as the ability and constancy of all Christians to be able to stand on their own, individually, thus missing the corporate essence of spiritual maturity according to the text.

Furthermore, from the text, the primary means of attaining spiritual maturity is the participation of all Christians as started off and continuously equipped and guided by the ministers Christ appointed and gave to the church as gifts. In contradistinction, a majority of the church leaders understands the baptism and confirmation rites to be the primary means of attaining spiritual maturity. The church leadership also understands that spiritual maturity becomes complete when people accept Christ as their Lord and Saviour. With such understanding, the leadership of the church would be handicapped, or at least would not be motivated, with regard to developing effective spiritual growth programmes for the church.

Also, Ephesians 4:13–16 presents spiritual maturity as absolutely necessary and a lack of it as a dangerous state for the church to be in, but the church leaders' understanding of the necessity of spiritual maturity reflects lack of awareness about, an indifference to, or a naiveté about the fact that a church lacking spiritual maturity will likely succumb to the machinations of false teachers and other forces of error, who are resolved to deceive, mislead, and destroy. The implications of these findings for the work of the church are identified and presented.

1

Introduction

THE CHURCH IN AFRICA is often described as one mile wide and one inch deep. That means, whereas the church is widely spread, the depth of the faith of the believers is rather superficial and generally weak. This is indicated by the fact that many Christians engage in practices that are not consistent with biblical teaching, or they simply fail to be "salt and light" (Matt 5:13–16). But with regard to spiritual maturity, the church in Africa may not be an exception. Lack of spiritual maturity seems to be one of the major problems facing the global church. On the other hand, the church is mandated to evangelize, disciple, worship, and respond to the social and spiritual needs of society. Also, in order for any church to be alive, it must grow, or else it dies. Both of these aspects require not only a mature church but also a maturing church.

The author of Ephesians emphasizes that the church should become mature. He says that God has put in place the conditions for maturity, so that with such maturity the Ephesians would no longer be infants, tossed by the wind of every doctrine. The author seems to imply a particular level of maturity that the church is to reach, to grow out of the state of infancy. Therefore, Ephesians 4:13 seems to be a New Testament basis for striving to reach church maturity. There are other passages in the New Testament where the notion of growth or maturity for the church and individual believers is found.[1] However, Ephesians 4:13 is possibly the only passage in the New Testament where the ultimate goal of maturity is specified. A valid interpretation of this passage, which would lead to determining the meaning of Christian maturity, is therefore called for.

Since the New Testament books were written within a particular rhetorical tradition, interpreting New Testament pericopes requires both understanding the rhetorical conventions of the first readers and applying

1. Cf. Heb 5:11; 1 Pet 2:1–3.

a method of rhetorical criticism commensurate with the context of the first readers. An interpretation of a New Testament pericope would, therefore, necessitate an understanding of the rhetorical devices that the writer would have used and how the original readers would have interpreted the message. This implies that the interpretation of New Testament writings, hence, also Ephesians 4:1–16, should incorporate rhetorical approaches. A number of methods of rhetorical criticism exist,[2] but apparently these methods miss out one significant element, that is, the consideration of the first readers as distinct rhetorical communities whose rhetorical conventions would have been adopted by the writers of the New Testament texts. These methods were seemingly developed without first addressing a key meta-theoretical question of a socio-historic nature, namely, what rhetorical elements should be understood and incorporated in a method of rhetorical criticism for a New Testament passage?

Therefore, some pertinent questions need to be addressed: How should Christian maturity be understood in the light of Ephesians 4:1–16, and how can this understanding be used as a critical standard to evaluate the understanding and level of maturity of the church in a given context? Towards answering these questions, first a method of rhetorical criticism appropriate for interpreting Ephesians 4:1–16 is developed, then the communicative function of Ephesians 4:1–16 in the epistle is determined, after which Ephesians 4:13 is interpreted to determine the meaning of Christian maturity, more precisely, the dimensions of Christian maturity. Following a description of the understanding and level of spiritual maturity of the church in a specific context and exploring universal applicability, a critical evaluation and discussion is pursued in light of the meaning of maturity in Ephesians 4:1–16 and the state of the church from a maturity stand point.

The Epistle to the Ephesians presents, as one of its central themes, the meaning of Christian maturity and an implied exhortation to the church to strive for such maturity. The definition of a mature church according to Ephesians 4:13 forms a valid basis for evaluating the understanding and level of maturity of the church in a given context.

This is a rhetorical-critical study of Ephesians 4:13 and its implications for the life of the church. A rhetorical-critical approach will be used to study, interpret, and draw the implications of this particular passage. Since this study focuses on interpreting a particular New Testament passage

---

2. Such as those by Kennedy, *New Testament Interpretation*; Andrews, *Practice*; Mack, *Rhetoric*; and Cornelius, "Effectiveness."

Introduction

using the rhetorical criticism approach, it is deemed important to discuss rhetorical criticism itself in relation to New Testament interpretation, with a view to proposing an appropriate method of rhetorical criticism to be applied to interpret the text. Our view is that rhetorical criticism is an approach of which one finds various methods.

Following this introduction, chapter 2 looks at rhetorical criticism as a New Testament hermeneutic. In chapter 3, I examine the communicative function of Ephesians 4:1–16, followed by a presentation of an interpretation of Ephesians 4:13 in chapter 4. Chapter 5 presents a discussion based on a basic field research on spiritual maturity and the African church, with a reference to clergy and leaders in a specific context as a case study of Christian spiritual maturity in the church. In chapter 6 I identify and discuss the implications of the meaning of spiritual maturity in Ephesians 4:13 for the church today, including drawing key lessons from the case study. Chapter 7 is the conclusion of the book, in which two important questions are addressed and specific recommendations made.

2

Rhetorical Criticism in New Testament Hermeneutics

2.1 Introduction

THE PURPOSE OF THIS chapter is to develop an appropriate method of rhetorical criticism. New Testament hermeneutics is briefly discussed, basically to delineate its essence, assert its necessity, appreciate pertinent issues, and examine particular considerations in interpreting the New Testament epistles. Thereafter, rhetorical criticism is examined in terms of its efficacy for biblical interpretation, especially the New Testament, and various methods of rhetorical criticism. From the discussion on New Testament hermeneutics on the one hand, and rhetorical criticism on the other, a method to be applied to interpret Ephesians 4:13 is proposed.

2.2 New Testament Hermeneutics

Hermeneutics, a method of textual analysis, and historically associated with the interpretation of biblical texts, pertains to the process of exposing hidden meanings or understood as the science and art of biblical interpretation. The term "hermeneutics" possibly originated from Hermes, the name of the Greek deity who supposedly served as a messenger for other deities, transmitting and interpreting their communications to their respective recipients, both fortunate and unfortunate. According to Thompson, hermeneutics was "derived from the Greek verb, ἑρμηνεύω, ‹to interpret,› and from the noun, ἑρμηνεία, ‹interpretation.›"[1] One aspect of hermeneutics would be the study of the rules that govern interpretation of

1. Thompson, "Hermeneutic Inquiry," 230.

the entire biblical text. This is general hermeneutics, and it would include historical-cultural, contextual, lexical-syntactical, and theological analyses. However, within the biblical text, there are various genres such as parables, allegories, types, prophecy, narratives, poetry, and letters. There are rules that govern the interpretation of such genres, the study of which constitutes special hermeneutics. A blending of critical social theory and hermeneutics has resulted in a methodology of critical hermeneutics, a methodology that emphasizes an interpretation of language, as well as silence, while also situating the text and the interpreter in their socio-cultural traditions.

2.2.1 Necessity of New Testament Hermeneutics

Several blocks are likely to inhibit spontaneous understanding of the original meaning of a biblical passage, because of the socio-historic gap between the original readers of the text and all others at different places and times in history. The cultural and linguistic gaps between the first recipients and all others at other times and places also constitute blocks to spontaneous understanding of biblical texts. The original primary languages of the biblical text—Hebrew and Aramaic—have very different structures and idioms from those of Cigogo, English, Kiswahili, Afrikaans, or any other modern day languages. The translations do not always convey the full, complete, or exact meaning of the texts as intended in the original languages. Furthermore, there is a philosophical gap between the first readers of the biblical texts and all others since then. The first recipients had their own concepts of the universe and circumstances and their own view of life, different from those of all others. Therefore, as Virkler well sums it up, "Hermeneutics is needed, then, because of the historical, cultural, linguistic, and philosophical gaps that block a spontaneous, accurate understanding of God's word."[2]

2.2.2 Hermeneutical Issues in New Testament interpretation

Critical to New Testament interpretation is adapting an acceptable viewpoint with regard to some key issues, and acknowledging this viewpoint. One key issue in contemporary hermeneutics concerns the extent to which words in biblical texts are to be interpreted literally, figuratively, or symbolically. The continuum entails generally taking Scripture literally, at the

2. Virkler, *Hermeneutics*, 20.

one end, and considering many biblical accounts such as the Fall, the Flood, and the account of Jonah as allegories, symbols, or metaphors rather than historical events, at the other. In this respect, hermeneutical problems would arise where a reader takes a biblical account, word, or phrase in a different manner than the author intended. Thus, for example, much of the author's intended meaning in a given text would be distorted or even missed if a reader interprets the text literally where the author intended it to be figurative, and vice versa. A useful guiding principle is to identify clues from the syntax and the context to determine the sense in which particular accounts, words, or phrases are to be interpreted. This in turn requires an understanding of the socio-historical context in relation to the particular passage.

Another issue in biblical hermeneutics pertains to the role of spiritual factors in the perceptual process of the interpreter. The concern here is the extent to which, if at all, spiritual factors affect the ability of the interpreter to reach the correct meaning of the text and to perceive accurately the truths that are to be found in Scripture. One might argue that if two people are equally equipped to interpret biblical texts, the two would be equally effective interpreters. In contradistinction, it could be argued that spiritual commitment or lack of it would influence the ability to understand spiritual truth. However, it would seem that the principles of biblical interpretation, if followed—and they could be followed—by even a non-believer, would allow him or her understand the meaning. Also, if such principles are not followed by even an interpreter with sound spiritual qualities, the interpreter will not understand the meaning accurately, the spiritual qualities notwithstanding. Virkler presents a helpful resolve for this: that the unbeliever could intellectually comprehend many of the truths of Scripture using the same means of interpreting non-biblical texts, but he cannot truly know—act on and appropriate—these truths as long as he remains wanting in spiritual qualities.[3]

A third key issue is whether a biblical text would have only one valid meaning or possibly several valid meanings; and where a possibility of several valid meanings exists, whether multiple valid meanings are to be graded, to have some of them more valid than others. The general view that the meaning of a biblical text is what it means to the interpreter is questionable. I would argue that if the meaning of a text is removed from the author's intended meaning, there would be no determinate meaning, since no interpretation could correspond to the meaning of the text. This

---

3. See ibid.

would in turn mean that to banish the original author as the determiner of meaning is essentially to reject the only compelling normative principle that could lend validity to an interpretation.

It is my view that the goal of biblical interpretation is to determine as closely as possible what God meant in a particular passage. The meaning of every passage would always be the same although the application could be different, depending on the specific circumstances of the interpreter. Without such a view, and instead, presuming the meaning of a particular biblical text to be what it means to the interpreter would imply that each passage in the Bible may have as many meanings as there are interpreters. This would, in turn, imply that there can be no distinction between orthodox and heretic interpretations of a given biblical text.

Double authorship of Scripture is another issue in contemporary hermeneutics. This refers to the possibility of a variation of meaning, perhaps in degree and scope, between the intentions of the human author and those of the Holy Spirit, the divine author. Since the *sensus plenior* debate is not likely to be concluded anytime soon, the orthodox view of confluent authorship of biblical texts is sufficient. That means the Holy Spirit directed the author, utilizing the author's particular personological characteristics, and the author collaborated with the Holy Spirit to write only that which—and in a manner that—the Holy Spirit intended in the context of the first recipients.

2.2.3 Hermeneutical Considerations with Regard to the Epistles

Since the focus of this study is a passage in an epistle—Ephesians—it is important to discuss briefly the basic hermeneutical considerations to be made in interpreting epistles. German scholar Herman Gunkel (1862–1932) advanced form criticism, in what he termed *Gattungsforschung*, that is, the investigation of types of literature. From his use of the concepts of genre (*Gattung*), form (*Form*), and setting in life (*Sitz im Leben*), Gunkel advanced a literary approach to the study of Scripture by focusing attention on identifying the genre of the text in the process of interpretation. From Gunkel's influential thinking, form criticism (*Formgeschichte*) emerged, particularly in New Testament studies, and genre is to be found as one of the key topics in form criticism. Genre in Gunkel's view referred to literary types, identifiable on the basis of content, mood, and linguistic form. Along this understanding, epistles are generally accepted, considered, and treated as belonging to a genre of their own kind. Fee and Stuart, for example, devote two chapters to discuss hermeneutical considerations in regard to epistles as a particular genre.[4]

In interpreting epistles, it is necessary to understand and recognize the nature of epistles, particularly, the fact that in spite of the possible differences among them, the crucial matter that is common to all epistles is that they are all occasional documents. That means the epistles arose out of, and were intended for, specific occasions during the first century. It further means that although the writing of the epistles was inspired by the Holy Spirit and, hence, the epistles were written for all people of all times everywhere, they were nevertheless written to particular first readers. The occasional nature of the epistles must be taken seriously, because epistles were called forth by some special circumstance, either from the reader's side or from the author's, often seeking to correct some behavior or some doctrinal error, or providing authoritative guidance on some misunderstanding. In addition, the occasional nature of the epistles means that they were not intended to expound Christian theology as such, although there is theology implied.

The occasional nature of epistles has critical implications for how they are to be interpreted. In particular, the interpretation of epistles requires an examination of the historical context in and for which a particular epistle was written, in order to possibly determine the occasion or the issues the author is seeking to address. The interpretation will also require an examination of the literary context, to accurately trace the author's primary argument in the epistle.

Interpretation of epistles also requires an understanding of the letter tradition of the first century[5]. Early letter writing was carried out in order to maintain communication between kings and is often referred to as "diplomatic" correspondence. Royal correspondence was also used to convey military orders or transmit reports, and letters could be used to address issues of management of internal affairs. Postal service was first developed in Mesopotamia in the sixth century BC, but it was used for official purposes,

---

4. See Fee & Stuart, *How to Read*.

5. White ("Ancient Greek Letters") presents an excellent essay in which he provides useful historical background to the ancient Greek letters and their influence on the Christian letters. Furthermore, as Richards (*Paul and First-Century Letter Writing*, 13–17, 32–4) indicates, Ancient Greece letter writing process involved a number of people, including secretaries.

and ordinary citizens from that time through the end of the Roman Empire had no organized delivery system available to them.

Once the letter form had developed to the point that it was not dependent on a messenger to supply parts of its formulae, a fairly standard arrangement of topics, found even in letters from the ancient Near East in Cuneiform or Aramaic, was set. The major parts of a letter were the opening,[6] the body, which contained those topics that express the purpose of the letter, and the closing. The discovery in the late nineteenth century in Egypt of thousands of private letters written on papyrus provided a source of non-literary, private correspondence for scholars to analyze. Private letters were used typically to handle business matters and to maintain lines of communication with families. If one were illiterate, one could turn to secretaries who could transcribe one's message and would include a formula of authentication to guarantee that the recipient would view the secretary's work as a reliable expression of the intent of the author.

In the Greek papyrus letter tradition, there are formulaic words or phrases associated with each section of the letter. The simplest form of greeting consists of three words—two if the name of the sender is left off—namely, the name of the sender in the nominative case, the recipient in the dative, and the infinitive form of the verb "greet." The greeting could be elaborated by adding attributive terms to the names, such as phrases to indicate family kinship or relationships, or by qualifying the verb.

In general, letters fell under the categories of friendship, family, praise or blame, hortatory, mediation, and apologetic, and they would be private or official and literary or non-real letters. Depending on the type of letter, the body may be introduced with the use of a disclosure formula or some expression of knowledge shared by the correspondents or an event experienced by them that the writer wants to make sure the recipient remembers.[7]

The single most characteristic formula of the letter closing was the use of the equivalent word for "farewell," which when used in the final

---

6. The opening contains the greeting, which usually identifies the sender and recipient, and a word of greeting. This is usually followed immediately by a "health wish," which typically expresses hope for the good health of the recipient, undergirded by assurances that the sender has offered prayers in support of that hope. Expressions of joy or frustration, both of which act to maintain contact by reminding the recipient of an earlier circumstance shared by the sender and recipient, are sometimes substituted for the health wish (see Amador, *Academic Constraints*; White, "Ancient Greek Letters," 89–97).

7. See for example, Paul's phrases such as "You know..." (1 Thess 2:1), "I want you to know..." (Rom 1:13; Phil 1:12); and "we do not want you to be ignorant..." (2 Cor 1:8).

greetings would also function as a kind of extension of the health wish. Another common term is "prosper," which implied a hope for the welfare of the recipient. In some letters, however, the closing could serve as a kind of epilogue that summarizes or restates the major topics found in the body, and might also contain greetings for persons other than the recipient and, occasionally, a date.

2.2.4 Rhetorical Criticism and New Testament Studies

Rhetorical criticism is becoming more and more recognized as a method of interpretation of Pauline as well as other parts of biblical literature. At the beginning of the 1990s many biblical interpretation scholars felt that biblical rhetorical criticism offered a methodological hybrid that meant a more vibrant strain of scholarship, benefiting from the crossing of diverse branches of knowledge. The integration of biblical and rhetorical studies has yielded the new hybrid of interpretation—rhetorical criticism. It is clear that rhetorical criticism is more than mere stylistic analyses, social descriptions, or historical reconstructions. Andrews views rhetorical criticism as the process of focussing attention on human efforts to persuade;[8] it regards the speech as an act of communication with a specific audience,[9] and holds as its business the analysis and appreciation of the orator's method of imparting his ideas to the hearers. The question to begin with, however, is whether in fact rhetorical criticism can serve as a hermeneutical approach to interpreting biblical texts. In the following sections, this matter is examined.

Some biblical scholars have expressed reservations about the application of rhetorical criticism in biblical studies. For example, Amador, in his *Academic Constraints of Rhetorical Criticism*, offers perhaps the most consolidated dissenting voice regarding the applicability of the rhetorical criticism approach to biblical studies in general and, apparently, New Testament interpretation in particular. He traces what he considers helpful but predictably constrained resurgence of rhetorical methods in biblical studies since James Muilenburg's 1968 presidential address[10] at the annual meeting

---

8. Andrews, *Practice*, 3ff.

9. The designation "audience" is used deliberately, as opposed to "receiver," in recognition of the fact that the target of communication is always involved in processing the incoming message cues or signals, and not passively receiving them.

10. See Muilenberg, "Form Criticism and Beyond."

of the Society of Biblical Literature. He criticizes the "causalist assumption" of modernist biblical scholarship, which operates as if there were a more or less direct correspondence between rhetorical "texts" and the "real or genuine" historical contexts and audiences to which they were addressed.[11]

However, the relevance and appropriateness of rhetorical criticism to biblical hermeneutics are apparent. For example, Meynet's primary purpose in *Rhetorical Analysis* is to persuade the reader that the biblical text follows identifiable rhetorical techniques, namely, parallelism and concentric "chiastic" structures. His conviction is that an awareness of these literary elements is an important key for understanding the message of particular passages, sections, and even entire books of the Bible. In the introduction (pp. 37–42) Meynet argues that these techniques reflect the "specific organizational laws of biblical texts" and that they are characteristic of the cultural milieu that produced the Scriptures. Meynet attempts to surface what is inherent in the biblical material itself.

In Part I of the book (chs. 1–3), Meynet traces the same sort of textual observations done by others since the eighteenth century, to demonstrate that his textual observations are neither totally new nor eccentric.[12] In Part II of the book (chs. 4–8) he explains the components of "rhetorical analysis" with multiple examples drawn from the entire Bible. The conclusion (pp. 351–59) briefly summarizes the work and then offers a few additional examples drawn from Ugaritic, Akkadian, and Islamic texts. In Part II he offers a detailed systematic presentation of the techniques of parallelism and concentric structures in the Bible. Chapter 4 presents his foundational presuppositions. Meynet summarizes his argument, saying: "If it were necessary to synthesize in one formula the whole of those presuppositions, I would say that *the biblical texts are well composed, if they are analyzed according to the laws of biblical rhetoric, and the study of their composition enables one to understand them better, as far as the analysis brings to light*

---

11. Amador, *Academic Constraints*, 27–29, 31.

12. Here Meynet (*Rhetorical Analysis*) surveys other authors who were cognizant of these techniques, basically highlighting the work of a few authors in each of the last three centuries. In the eighteenth century the pioneer would have been Robert Lowth in England, who pointed out the ubiquitousness of parallelism in Hebrew poetry and categorized it into several basic types (ch. 1). In the nineteenth century, he presents John Jebb, who also focused on parallelism and to some extent chiastic structures, and Thomas Boys, presumably the first to give extensive attention to chiasm throughout the Bible (ch. 2). The most important person of the twentieth century would have been Nils Wilhelm Lund, who presumably rediscovered and expanded the rhetorical techniques (ch. 3).

their inner logic."[13] In his second presupposition, Meynet states that "there is a specifically biblical rhetoric."[14]

This means that biblical scholars are to train themselves to discern the inner logic of coherent and well-crafted biblical texts. The wide variety of kinds of each technique Meynet explains in chapters 5 and 6. Chapter 7 explains how this approach can be visualized by textual rewrites and diagrams. Meynet sees four principal fruits of this sort of analysis (ch. 8). First, attention to details can help to better delimit literary units. Second, this study can aid in the interpretation of texts, since "form is the gateway to meaning." Third, rhetorical analysis can assist the translator in being alert for key terms and more respectful of syntactic structures. Finally, this approach can inform the task of textual criticism by granting more credence to the final form of the text; difficulties can sometimes be solved by consideration of structure.

For anyone interested in more literary approaches to biblical studies, Meynet's work provides useful insights and applicable tools for a closer observation of the text. For our purposes here, Meynet acknowledges the usefulness and implies the possibility of rhetorical analysis of biblical texts. Similarly, Trible in her *Rhetorical Criticism* quite successfully applies rhetorical criticism to study the Book of Jonah. Thus, generally, rhetorical criticism is becoming more and more recognized as an approach to interpretation of biblical texts. The Pepperdine Conferences provide a fuller evidence of the efficacy of rhetorical criticism as an approach to biblical hermeneutics, as the review below suggests. Many other biblical studies scholars either acknowledge or imply the usefulness or relevance of the rhetorical criticism approach to interpreting biblical texts.[15] Some scholars link applicability of the rhetorical criticism approach to the epistles or to Paul's writings or speeches,[16] or specifically to the Epistle to the Ephesians.[17]

James Muilenburg's presidential address at the 1968 conference of the Society of Biblical Literature remains perhaps one of the most significant influences towards embracing rhetorical criticism in biblical studies,

---

13. Meynet, *Rhetorical Analysis*, 169 (emphasis original).

14. Ibid., 172.

15. See for example Robbins, "Present and Future" and "Argumentative Textures"; Bloomquist, "Role of the Audience."

16. Examples of these include Holland, "Paul's Use of Irony"; Porter, "Ancient Rhetorical Analysis"; Ericksson, "Contrary Arguments."

17. See for example Jeal, "Rhetorical Argumentation"; Lemmer, "Rhetoric and Metaphor."

particularly New Testament studies. In his paper, Muilenburg both appreciated the strengths of the form criticism approach but also went beyond the hitherto narrow focus on individual pericopes, characteristically to the exclusions of the "individual, personal and unique features," observing that one would want to supplement form-critical analysis with careful inspection of the literary unit in its precise and unique formulation. Thus, in Muilenburg's view, rhetorical criticism was required to supplement form criticism. Criticizing the tendency of traditional form criticism to fixate on conventions, slight historical commentary, separate form from content, isolate and focus on small units, and resist psychological and biographical interpretation, Muilenburg pointed out the need to pay attention to and incorporate in biblical interpretation structural patterns, verbal sequences, and stylistic devices that made a passage coherent. Muilenburg named this endeavor "rhetoric" and its methodology "rhetorical criticism." For Muilenburg, a responsible and proper articulation of the words in their linguistic patterns and in their precise formulations would reveal the texture and fabric of the writer's thought, "not only what he thinks, but as he thinks it."

A number of issues has been raised with regard to the Muilenburg program. Trible provides a good summary of scholarly critique of the Muilenburg's proposal.[18] First, Muilenburg misses the need to include the persuasion element, a primary aspect to be found in all major traditional angles of rhetorical theory. A method of studying a biblical text in terms of its stylistic-aesthetic features to the exclusion or disregard of its persuasive potency or intent would not qualify as rhetorical criticism. Furthermore, Muilenburg tends to separate the text from its context and fails to address the concepts of diachronic and synchronic readings of the text. These issues notwithstanding, Muilenburg's contribution to the development of rhetorical criticism as an approach to the study of the biblical text is quite significant. The subject of rhetoric within biblical studies has since become a full-fledged methodology practiced in different ways.[19] From this assertion, three emphases are apparent: rhetoric signifies the art of composition, the method involves close reading of the text, and the purpose is to discover authorial intent. Even the task of the rhetoric critic is conceptualized: to define the limits of a literary unit using the criteria of form and content, and

---

18. See Trible, *Rhetorical Criticism*.

19. According to Trible (*Rhetorical Criticism*, 32) the differences in doing rhetorical criticism arise from understanding rhetoric as the art of composition or as the art of persuasion.

to discern structure by delineating the overall design of the individual parts and to show they work together and identify literary devices.

The number of key conferences on rhetoric and biblical interpretation organized during the 1990s[20] attests to the heightened interest on the subject. It is informative to summarize the focus of each of these conferences and their apparent contributions to the development of rhetorical criticism as an approach to biblical, especially New Testament interpretation.[21]

The primary focus of the Heidelberg 1992 conference was the history and theory of rhetoric and applications of rhetorical criticism to some New Testament books. Whereas seven essays focused on the history or theory of rhetoric, five papers focused on Luke-Acts, fourteen papers on Pauline epistles,[22] and one on Hebrews. There were also some essays on the biographical historiography and epistles in the New Testament using strategies that covered a spectrum from classical rhetorical interpretation to the new rhetorical criticism of Perelman and Olbrechts-Tyteca. At the Pretoria 1994 conference seven essays focused on theory, four on the Hebrew Bible, one on Acts, four on Pauline epistles,[23] one on 2 Peter, and one on *Acts of Thomas*. Elisabeth Schüssler Fiorenza's lead paper focused primarily on rhetorical situation and historical reconstruction in 1 Corinthians.

At the London 1995 rhetoric conference eleven essays were presented, on Pauline epistles: three on theoretical issues; two on Romans; four on 1 and 2 Corinthians; one on Philippians; and one on Titus.[24] Robbins lead-off essay, entitled "The Present and Future of Rhetorical Analysis," introduced socio-rhetorical interpretive analytics for interpreting Bible texts and explored the historical-ideological relation of Schüssler Fiorenza's commentary discourse on 1 Corinthians to Betz's commentary discourse on the Sermon on the Mount. In his reflections at the end of the conference, Jasper asserted that despite the recognition of the postmodern situation within which the papers had been written, the parameters of the project remained

---

20. These conferences were held at Heidelberg (1992), Pretoria (1994), London (1995), Malibu (1996), Florence (1998), Lund (2000), and Heidelberg (2002).

21. For an extended summary of the volumes produced from each of these conferences, see Robbins, "Rhetorical Analysis."

22. Five on theory, one on Acts and Paul's epistles, two on Romans, two on 1 Corinthians, one on 2 Corinthians, and three on Philippians.

23. One each on theory, 1 Thessalonians, Ephesians, and Colossians.

24. See Robbins, "Rhetorical Analysis."

The Mature Church

"comfortably lodged within the traditional critical limits of authorial intentionality and historical criticism."[25]

Among the key essays at the 1996 conference on rhetoric and biblical studies held at Pepperdine University's Malibu Campus[26] were Olbricht's "Classical Rhetorical Criticism and Historical Reconstructions: A Critique," Watson's "The Contributions and Limitations of Greco-Roman Rhetorical Theory for Constructing the Rhetorical and Historical Situations of a Pauline Epistle," Kota Yamada's "The Preface to the Lukan Writings and Rhetorical Historiography," Bloomquist's presentation of a socio-rhetorical analysis of Luke 21, and Stamps' exploration of the theological rhetoric of Pauline epistles. Robbins observes that in general the essays reflected the programmatic journeys the authors were taking through the strengths and limitations of classical rhetorical criticism, epistolography, rhetorical historiography, special topics in Christian literature, the functional grammar of Halladay, socio-rhetorical interpretation, the nature of theological rhetoric, and expressions of anger and reflections on self in ancient texts.[27]

The primary focus of the Florence 1998 conference was the rhetorical analysis of Scripture.[28] At least ten of the papers presented at that conference reflected a growing interest in the tapestry of socio-rhetorical criticism, indicating an apparent shift to a rhetoric of how a text constructs a new sociology of being.

The Lund 2000 Conference focused primarily on argumentation and all the papers presented there had some aspects of argumentation. Included were such papers as Vernon Robbins' "Argumentative Textures in Socio-Rhetorical Interpretation," Dean Anderson's "Is There Biblical Argumentation?," and Carol Poster's "The Economy of Letter Writing in Graeco-Roman Antiquity." But also, there were two essays on the Hebrew Bible (Chronicles, 1 Kings 22), four on the Gospels, including Attridge's analysis of argumentation in John 5, nine essays on Paul's letters, one on Hebrews, and one on the Acts of Peter.

---

25. Jasper, "Reflections," 476.
26. See Robbins, "Rhetorical Analysis."
27. Ibid.
28. Porter & Stamps, *Rhetorical Criticism*, 9.

2.2.5 Summary

In general, there has been growing interest in understanding and applying rhetorical criticism as an approach to biblical interpretation. The approach is applicable and useful to biblical interpretation, not because there has been much interest in it, and not even because there has been considerable wide application of the same, but because the arguments presented or implied suggest so. The concern may be one of the extent to which rhetorical criticism as an approach is correctly integrated with other techniques of interpreting biblical texts. Reviewed literature does not acknowledge or clarify that rhetorical criticism is to be understood, among other things, as an approach. It is, however, my view that rhetorical criticism is an approach with a number of possible methods, since there is not one but any number of methods of rhetorical criticism.

Interest in using methods of rhetorical criticism has led to articulation and use of more methods of rhetorical criticism. The next section examines these methods of rhetorical criticism with a view to appraising them and suggesting aspects of possible extension of the rhetorical criticism approach to New Testament interpretation.

2.3 Methods of New Testament Rhetorical Criticism: An Appraisal

This section appraises selected methods of rhetorical criticism thus far used in New Testament interpretation and, subsequently, proposes an extension of the rhetorical criticism approach. Particular attention is given to Kennedy's method because of its significant place in the literature on rhetorical criticism as an approach to New Testament interpretation, but other methods are also examined. Upon this appraisal of the selected methods of rhetorical criticism, an alternative method of rhetorical criticism is proposed.

Several methods of rhetorical criticism exist such as those proposed by Mack, Andrews, and Cornelius.[29] However, perhaps the more widely known and, possibly, the most influential so far is the method of rhetorical criticism proposed by Kennedy. It is, therefore, deemed necessary to discuss Kennedy's method as a starting point.

---

29. Mack, *Rhetoric*; Andrews, *Practice*; Cornelius, "Effectiveness."

2.3.1 Kennedy's Method of Rhetorical Criticism

Kennedy's relevant works, namely, *Classical Rhetoric and Its Christian and Secular Tradition from Ancient to Modern Times* (1980) and *New Testament Interpretation through Rhetorical Criticism* (1984), show that Kennedy's approach to rhetorical criticism is premised on his definition of early Christian rhetoric. Presuming that certain aspects of the Jewish world gave birth to early Christianity and its rhetoric, Kennedy interprets Mark 13:9–13 and 1 Corinthians 1:22–2:13 and, subsequently, forms the basis of his definition of early Christian rhetoric. Kennedy draws a disjuncture between early Christian rhetoric and classical rhetoric: "Christian preaching is thus not persuasion, but proclamation, and is based on authority and grace, not on proof." This definition hinges on two New Testament passages. Of the first, Mark 13:9–13, Kennedy writes:

> Among the points to be noted in this passage are the importance of testimony up to and including the example of martyrdom; the fact that no special eloquence is required, for as in Exodus God will provide the words; and an apparent assumption that the disciples cannot expect to persuade their judges of the righteousness of their cause: that is God's work, and as with Pharaoh, he seems to intend to harden their hearts. All of this is completely contrary to the situation of the classical orator, who uses eloquence to overcome enormous opposition in defence of himself and his clients.[30]

In his *New Testament Interpretation through Rhetorical Criticism*, Kennedy includes a similar definition of early Christian rhetoric. On the basis of references to the Holy Spirit in Mark 13:11 and 1 Corinthians 2:13, Kennedy makes an inference that the Holy Spirit is the source of early Christian rhetoric. He contends that

> The Christian orator, like his Jewish predecessor, is a vehicle of God's will to whom God will supply the necessary words, and his audience will be persuaded, or not persuaded, not because of the capacities of their minds to understand the message, but because of God's love for them which allows their hearts to be moved or withholds that grace.[31]

Kennedy's view that classical rhetoric and early Christian rhetoric were different phenomena, as proposed in 1980, would render interpretation of

---

30. Kennedy, *Classical Rhetoric*, 127.
31. Kennedy, *New Testament Interpretation*, 8.

the New Testament through rhetorical criticism irrelevant, since one could not apply rhetorical criticism to texts which utilized proclamation rather than classical modes of persuasion. But his later books somewhat make a modification of his earlier definition of early Christian rhetoric, limiting the definition to texts he designates "radical Christian rhetoric."[32] Kennedy explains that these radical texts, which originate with the Holy Spirit, are different from New Testament texts which utilize classical modes of persuasion.[33] Thus, there exist three categories, namely, classical rhetorical persuasion, early Christian rhetoric utilizing classical rhetorical persuasion, and the radical Christian rhetoric. To the final category belongs, not the totality of early Christian rhetoric, as his prior book suggests, but only some of it, such as the Gospel of Mark.

Kennedy contends that while Greek oratory was more logical than in the case of religious discourse, it contained nevertheless a good deal of appeal to current values and opinions with logical arguments often only introduced to give a semblance of reason.[34] By contrast, in religious discourse the premises of arguments are usually based on divine authority, often mediated by scriptural quotation, and on personal intuition. However, Kennedy does not provide a complete set of criteria for distinguishing the two types of early Christian rhetoric. The basic criteria for discerning radical Christian rhetoric seem to be absence of enthymemes. The second difficulty becomes apparent when Kennedy subjects the Gospel of Mark to rhetorical analysis. On the one hand, he regards it as an expose of radical Christian rhetoric; on the other hand, he discovers enthymemes in it.

It is unlikely that early Christian rhetoric was really so free from persuasion as Kennedy's definition suggests. Kennedy relates the developing internal rhetoric of Christianity to the traditions of Judaism, implying that Jewish texts could provide significant data for evaluating the veracity of his definition of early Christian rhetoric.[35] A review of early Jewish texts that antedate 135 BC exposes two traditions that provide a backdrop for radical Christian rhetoric and its foundational texts of Mark 13:9–13 and 1 Corinthians 1–2. The first tradition presents the Spirit as the power that overcomes the speaker, as expressed in the writings of Philo and Josephus, whereby it is understood that prophetic speech occurs when the prophet

32. Ibid., 7.
33. Ibid., 104.
34. See both *Classical Rhetoric* and *New Testament Interpretation*.
35. See his *Classical Rhetoric*.

is overcome by the Spirit, that is, when the prophet ceases to be conscious. Prophetic rhetoric, then, is produced not by reason but by the Spirit through the medium of a prophet who is unaware of this inspiration. The other tradition presents the Spirit as the Artificer, and sees Spirit-inspired rhetoric as the equipping by the Spirit for the wise person to be intelligent in thought and, consequently, persuasive in speech. The basis for this viewpoint is the conviction that the Spirit is a Spirit of wisdom and intelligence. The implication, then, is that truly inspired rhetoric belongs not to the spiritually overcome individual but to the diligent scribe.

This survey of early Judaism supplies ample evidence for Kennedy's contention that the earliest believers expected God to supply the words and to accomplish persuasion. But equally likely, it also provides abundant evidence for an alternative argument, namely, that the earliest believers may have expected the Spirit to guide their study and their preparation for speaking. To evaluate which viewpoint is more likely to have been the case, one might need to examine the two New Testament passages that provide the foundation for Kennedy's definition of early Christian rhetoric. After such an analysis, Levison concludes that Kennedy's definition of radical Christian rhetoric draws "too radical a distinction between the Spirit and rhetoric, between Christian preaching as proclamation and Christian preaching as persuasion."[36] Furthermore, even if early Christian rhetoric was different from secular rhetoric, which it was, the grounds provided by Kennedy for that difference are nonsupportive as they cannot themselves be supported.

Anyhow, in his contribution to rhetorical analysis of New Testament texts, Kennedy presents a five-step method of rhetorical criticism.[37] First, one should determine the rhetorical unit to be analyzed. Then, it is necessary to define the rhetorical situation in terms of the exigency involved. Third, the rhetorical unit may be analyzed in terms of the classical statis theory, that is, the basic issue of the central question involved. Fourth, the analysis should determine the species of rhetoric or rhetorical genre to which the rhetorical unit belongs, that is, whether the forensic, deliberative, or epideictic genre. After these preliminary matters have been attended, the critic then turns to the analysis of the arrangement of material in terms of the subdivisions of the discourse, the persuasive effects of these parts, and how they work together in achieving or not achieving a unified purpose in

---

36. Levison, "Did the Spirit Inspire Rhetoric?," 40.
37. Kennedy, *New Testament Interpretation*, 33–38.

meeting the rhetorical situation. This will involve a line-by-line analysis of arguments in the light of assumptions, topics, formal features, and devices of style.

By way of evaluation, more than anything, Kennedy's main contribution is methodological, as he presents a distinctive method that is lucid and systematic. His approach to a text is purely rhetorical. Approaching a letter as an argument, he considers the methods of persuasion in the various parts of the argument and determines their functions. His analysis of the rhetorical situation entails mainly the audience and the rhetorical problem faced by the writer. He therefore intends to explain the form of communication by means of the rhetorical situation and to read the text in the same way as it would be read by the first readers.

Kennedy's important contribution above notwithstanding, several flaws can be identified. First, Kennedy allows and follows the rhetorical genres proposed by Aristotle as sufficiently general and inclusive in character to be universally applicable. It was the forensic (judicial), deliberative (political), and epideictic (ceremonial) genres systematized by Aristotle that became a standard part of Greco-Roman rhetoric.[38] Neo-Aristotelian criticism focuses on the effects of the artefact on the audience and whether the rhetor selected the best strategies for achieving the intended effects.

Second, the anomalous character of Aristotle's classification has long been recognized with regard to the types of audience characterized for each genre. Aristotle's classification was, it seems, an attempt to cover the existing fields of oratory of his day and consequently it can only be defended from those circumstances.[39] Thus, the forensic and deliberative genres must be seen as rooted in the political and judicial types of rhetorical contexts of Aristotle's time. As such, they will only be useful in categorizing speeches that reflect more or less the same types of rhetorical contexts. With regard to epideictic genre, the generality of the audience of this genre and its varying celebrative contexts (e.g., funerals, festivals, sophistic exercises) led to divergence and confusion among subsequent theorists, and ultimately, it became a repository for all types of speeches and other literary forms that could not be subsumed under the other two.

Third, even if the view were granted, that Aristotle's classification could apply transhistorically, the classification would not be valid for

---

38. See *Rhet* 1.3.1–5 in Aristotle, *Rhetoric*, 7–22; also see Hill, "Aristotle's Rhetorical Theory."

39. For an extended discussion on this see Mbennah, "Impact of Audience."

religious rhetoric generally and Christian rhetoric particularly. In an age not accustomed to sermons and where protreptics were most often heard in a political assembly, Aristotle simply did not consider the type of speech that could be both hortatory and delivered to spectators, as the case may be in much of religious discourse. Black argues convincingly that there is a type of rhetorical genre that lies outside of Aristotle's theory, "one in which the evocation of an emotional experience in the audience induces belief in the situation to which the emotion is appropriate instead of following as a consequence of belief in the situation."[40] Such a rhetoric follows procedures that do not find their end in judgement, but rather inculcate new convictions by obliterating the audience's capacity for making judgements. Thus, in the epistles, for example, in addressing religious audiences with regard to shared interests in pertinent beliefs and practices, the ultimate persuasive goal would be to strengthen continued adherence to the Christian gospel, whatever specific exigencies may occasion a particular letter. That is to say, in the case of New Testament texts one has to do with a basically different audience role than those of the legal judge, the political deliberator, or the spectator who does not need to take any particular decisive stand, in the Aristotelian position. Consequently, with regard to all genres, when Kennedy states that "although these categories specifically refer to the circumstances of classical civic oratory, they are in fact applicable to all discourse,"[41] it must be seen as a questionable methodological proposition. It would seem, then, that in Kennedy's rhetorical criticism criteria, historically conditioned genres are being treated as though they were universal, ahistorical types. No doubt there will be common features that meet on a higher level of generality, but a genre finds its definition in terms of a characteristic grouping of distinctive features that are usually appropriate to a particular type of communicative context.

And fourth, Aristotle's *Rhetoric*, upon which Neo-Aristotelianism was based, was not intended as a guide for critics. Rather, *Rhetoric* and other classical works that were being used were designed to teach others how to speak well, rather than to appraise discourse. Neo-Aristotelianism seems to exclude all evaluations other than the speech's potential for evoking intended response from the immediate, specified audience. Still, the Neo-Aristotelian approach would be criticized on the grounds that *Rhetoric* and its other classical bases were written in a different socio-historic context.

40. Black, *Rhetorical Criticism*, 118.
41. Kennedy, *New Testament Interpretation*, 19.

Neo-Aristotelianism has also been criticized for its rational bias. A basic assumption of the method is that the unique attribute of human beings is the capacity and tendency to be rational, and that human beings are able to engage in persuasion and be subject to it because they are rational beings.

2.3.2 Trible's Method of Rhetorical Criticism

In her book *Rhetorical Criticism: Context, Method, and the Book of Jonah*, Phyllis Trible applies a particular approach to rhetorical criticism in analyzing the Book of Jonah, an approach worthy noting. In the first part of the book, Trible covers matters of context—providing a background sketch, introducing the foreground, and expanding the background. In the second and last part of the book, Trible develops a method and applies it to interpret the Book of Jonah. According to Trible, classical rhetoric, literary critical theory, literary study of the Bible, and form criticism continue to provide the context in which biblical rhetorical criticism takes place.[42] Trible observes that in the modern sense of form criticism, "form" refers to structure and genre together, the former designating the outline of the text, and the latter specifying the type of literature. Also, the relationship between the genre and the setting expands, going beyond the institutions, to include "linguistic milieu," literary connections, aesthetic features, psychological framework, specific occasions, or even the general spirit of a place and time. All such variables, not just institutional phenomena, may shape genre. Furthermore, a particular setting does not determine or dictate a particular genre. The latter may enjoy multiple settings even as the former embrace multiple genres.[43]

Articulation of form-content. Trible says that the hyphenated construction shows the organic unity of form and content while at the same time acknowledging the ingredients. "Form" in form-content in rhetorical criticism designates only the structure (as opposed to both structure and genre in traditional form criticism). In addition, "structure" as designated by "form" refers not to the topical outline of the passage but to the patterns of relationships residing in the very words, sentences, phrases, and larger units. The form-content separation is only to facilitate recognition of the ingredients, but the two are inseparable, as both what a text says and how it says together give meaning. In this regard, form in and of the text

---

42. Trible, *Rhetorical Criticism*, 55.
43. Ibid., 82.

is considered particular to that text. In this regard, articulation of form-content raises issues about the relationship between the text and the larger world. Rhetorical criticism belongs to the intrinsic approach, whereby the focus is on the text, and not on the external factors such as historical data, authorial intention, sociological setting, or theological milieu. Trible posits that in analyzing the extrinsic, for example, by forging explicit connections among a single text, other texts, and the larger environment, articulation of form-content remains primary, environment secondary.

Articulation of meaning. Meaning pertains to variety—with author, text, and audience meaning. Authorial meaning refers to the meaning the human author of the text would have intended to communicate or generate in the audience—the fabric of the author's thought. In this sense, there is acknowledgment of the existence of author's intent and a particular way the author "attempts" to convey that meaning. There are, of course, difficult questions that one could raise: Would literature be a window through which to see the author's mind? Would meaning be restricted to authorial intent? Is it not possible for the literature to speak differently than the author's intention? What is the connection between the human author and the divine author, in the case of biblical texts? The difficulty of these questions notwithstanding, texts reveal authors in terms of their experiences, social backgrounds, knowledge, resources, perspectives, and skills. However, authorial intention would constitute only a part of the total meaning of the text.

According to Trible, textual meaning, separable from the author's intention, is constituted by the content, the interlocking structures, and artistic configurations of a text, not quite intended or completely in the control of the author.[44] This implies recognition of the limits of language as well as the power of language to specify and signify. One has to contend with some crucial questions in this regard: Can texts have a life of their own, separate from their authors? Do texts in fact have power? Aren't texts products of the society? Could texts be personified? Nonetheless, meaning inherent in the text ought not be discarded or disregarded because of these difficult questions.

Also, Trible is of the view that there is reader's meaning, whereby the reader of the text is presumed to describe the structure, style, and substance of the supposedly silent text, and thereby produce multiple renditions, depending on their knowledge, skills, abilities, and sensitivities to the

---

44. Ibid., 97.

interpretive process as well as the respective settings in which the reader engages with the text. In the case of biblical texts, there would be some good questions to wrestle with: Does "reader" refer to the first reader or the current reader, or any reader for that matter? Is meaning of a text then indefinitely flexible but still valid?

Trible then provides "practical instruction" in applying rhetorical criticism to interpreting biblical texts, with the following key steps:

- Beginning with the text, by reading and reading again and interacting with various sources, to understand the content and text, jotting any questions that come to mind as one reads the text.
- Reading various scholarly works on the text and making notes, from as many perspectives and formats as one can find.
- Surrounding the study of the text with background knowledge to give depth and perspective.
- Acquainting oneself with the rhetorical terms.
- Attending closely to the beginning and ending; repetition of words, phrases and sentences (thereby beginning to discern the structures and meanings); types of discourse, design and structure, observing plot development, character portrayals; and syntax and particles.
- Showing structure by using the very words of the text in the order they occur.
- Translating it so as to retain not only the syntax in the original language but also the original number of words.
- Devising a series of markers, to indicate prominent features of the text, especially repetition.
- Correlating one's discoveries, for example, how structural units relate to the plot development, or whether a particular unit interrupts the narrative flow in order to slow down action.[45]

By way of evaluation, Trible's method could be useful and applicable, especially the aspects of articulation of form-content and articulation of meaning. However, Trible's methods seems to focus primarily on the text and the process of analyzing a text and leaves out consideration of the original audience of the text, the rhetorical conventions of the time, and any particular rhetorical styles of the authors and any intentions to determine

45. Ibid., 101–6.

the authorial intended meaning. In the end, it seems that hers is simply a method of textual analysis, not a method of interpretation. In this respect it is quite debatable whether Trible's method is in fact a method of rhetorical criticism, as she intends.

2.3.3   Cornelius' Method of Rhetorical Criticism

Cornelius consults various theories and disciplines with a view to creating her own view of effective communication by means of a letter.[46] She is of the opinion that one does not criticize by finding illustrations of standard, preconceived forms; rather the critic must use the frameworks of standard techniques as norms to help one discover and evaluate ways in which the speaker's use of techniques is distinctive. The theory of rhetoric is thus used for practising rhetorical criticism. Cornelius' method of rhetorical criticism entails analysis, interpretation, and evaluation, with the first two aspects being the means to an end, which is evaluation. She focuses on the three components of a rhetorical act, namely, the author, text, and readers. Within this framework the following are done:

- Analysis and interpretation with a focus on the text
- Analysis and interpretation with a focus on the author
- Analysis and interpretation with a focus on the context
- Evaluation of the effectiveness of the rhetorical act

By way of evaluation, if the goal of analyzing a New Testament text is simply to understand what the text says to particular readers, rhetorically speaking, then this method is not only useful but also effective and essential. However, if the goal of the analysis is interpretation, of which the meaning of the text is key, then, strictly speaking, this is not a method of rhetorical criticism for New Testament interpretation, since it does not, as it were, aim or seek to obtain the meaning of the text.

2.4   Towards a Method of Rhetorical Criticism for New Testament Interpretation

The central theoretical argument of this section is that, whereas generally the rhetorical criticism approach is profitable for the interpretation of New

---

46. Cornelius, "Effectiveness."

Testament texts, such an approach would be valid only if it were developed around the view that the first readers of New Testament texts were a distinct rhetorical community, with its religious vocabulary, rhetorical visions, forms, styles, and conventions. It is not until one understands those forms and rhetorical styles as well as the socio-historic context of the early church and her views on sacred texts that one can adequately understand what God is speaking today through a given New Testament text. From a history of revelation point of view,[47] I presuppose that God spoke to his church and his world and I add that he did so through the rhetorical forms of the first readers of biblical texts. As such, for it to be valid, an appropriate method of rhetorical criticism needs to incorporate a construction of the socio-historic context of the first readers (especially its rhetorical forms and its way of handling sacred texts) and the construction of the rhetorical situations from which the texts arose.

2.4.1   A Theory of Rhetoric

Rhetorical criticism is a particular approach encompassing rhetoric and criticism. According to Croft, rhetorical theory as a basis for criticism would consist of a series of formal techniques drawn from the history of rhetorical theory and unified into a general system.[48] A theory of rhetoric would state the basic facts, central laws, and fundamental components of the rhetorical process. Brinton says a theory of rhetoric would be normative in nature and would be a fitting response to certain kinds of situations, hence it provides the basis for rhetorical criticism.[49] That implies that a method of rhetorical criticism would be premised on a particular theory of rhetoric. Hence, any critic has to spell out his theory of rhetoric, which is a theoretical framework arising from the critic's particular conceptualization of rhetoric for the purpose of rhetorical criticism and explanation of one's view of the rules and means of effective communication. It is in this regard that in this section a theory of rhetoric is articulated, from various sources of rhetorical traditions.

Generally, the development of rhetorical theory is indebted to the Athenian democracy in the fifth century BC, when in the popular assembly

---

47. For excellent discussions on history of revelation see Cullman, *Salvation History*; Ladd, *Theology*; Hasel, *New Testament Theology*.

48. Croft, "Functions," 414.

49. Brinton, "Situation," 239.

every male citizen had to make a contribution on issues to be decided by the Committee of the Five Hundred. As the process became increasingly important, responsibility of public statements was urgently called for, which resulted in a process of scrutinizing orators such that unworthy citizens would not speak in the assembly. They defined rhetoric as seeking to elicit a desired response in view of the orator's purpose. Since then, various conceptions of rhetoric or rhetorical theories have arisen. In the *Phaedrus*, Plato (born in 429 BC) argues, among other things, that good rhetoric must contain principles dealing with the arrangement of the materials and that the rhetorician should know the nature of the human soul and customize style and delivery to the particular audiences. Aristotle (384–322 BC), who defined rhetoric as the faculty of discovering the available means of persuasion in any subject, posited that rhetoric enables the speaker to maintain the truth against falsehood, advance discussion where definite proofs cannot be attained, expose irregularities in argument and see both sides of a controversy, and defend oneself with reason. According to Aristotle,[50] the most effective tool in argumentation is the enthymeme, a rhetorical syllogism that depends on the audience to supply one or more of the premises. The speaker has to discover and then create a syllogism that he is confident can be completed by the audience, who draw from their stock of knowledge either the major or minor premise to complete it, thus becoming persuaded because of the truth they recognize in the syllogism.

Cicero (106–43 BC), the most eminent of the orators of Roman civilization, a lawyer, successful politician, and a famous orator, remains the most prominent figure in the history of rhetoric. Cicero valued rhetoric so much that he wanted to make rhetoric part of the general culture, in which men would be trained to write and speak competently in all subjects. In 55 BC he composed *De Oratore*, his most important book on rhetorical theory. With a grant he received from Emperor Vespian (who ruled from AD 69), Cicero, possibly the greatest Latin authority on education, restored education at high levels to prepare young men for civil service. Cicero's view was that the proper concern of an orator is language of power and eloquence accommodated to the teachings and understandings of mankind. His position was that speech should be made becoming of its kind—complexion and substance of its own to be weighty, agreeable, savoring of erudition and liberal knowledge, worthy of admiration, polished, and having a feeling of passion in it. He held the view that speech should be strewn with flowers

---

50. See Aristotle, *Rhetoric*; Hill, "Aristotle's Rhetorical Theory," 93–99.

of language and thought as in arrangement of ornament. Cicero proposed the doctrine of the three styles—namely the plain, the moderate, and the grand—arising from the orator's attempts to prove, to please, or to move. Also, Quintilian's (AD 14–138) contribution to the development of rhetorical theory was quite significant, as particularly found in the *Institutes*.

The developments of rhetorical criticism from classical rhetorical theory were accelerated by Perelman and Olbrechts-Tyteca. In *The New Rhetoric: A Treatise on Argumentation*, they revive the Aristotelian thought, in which rhetoric was defined in terms of persuasion and the means of persuasion. They articulated a philosophy of argumentation in which they posited that, following agreed-upon principles of argumentation, the goal and end result of argumentation would be to establish a community of minds for debating issues and establish assent. Classical rhetoric recognized three parts of the rhetorical process, namely, speaker, speech and audience. Of these parts, Perelman and Olbrechts-Tyteca gave priority of place to the *relationship* of the speaker and the audience.

In general, rhetorical criticism concerns the interpretation and evaluation of a specific act of communication, which in turn suggests the objectives of rhetorical criticism to be describing or analyzing, interpreting, and evaluating a rhetorical act. Evaluation is seen as the central objective of a rhetorical-critical endeavor seeking to assess the extent to which, and the resources of rhetorical craftsmanship through which, the source achieves the end. Within these viewpoints, a key function of rhetorical criticism is to show how propositions and audiences are connected, how writers use techniques to adapt their ideas to those of their audiences, and what is actually communicated to the audience.

It appears then that the two primary reasons to engage in rhetorical criticism are both concerned with understanding rhetorical processes. One reason is to understand particular symbols and how they operate. As the critic comes to understand the workings of a particular artefact or act, he often also becomes involved in the social or ideological. The critic examines the worldview conveyed by a rhetorical artefact, the facts that are and are not acknowledged in the artefact, and the consequences and alternatives that it presents or ignores in light of moral, social, economic, and political issues.

However, in terms of the interpretation of biblical texts, viewing rhetorical criticism this way means that a biblical text would be taken as a rhetorical artefact and evaluated. It would seem to me that this would not be all that noble an objective. Therefore, a more prime function of rhetorical criticism applied to New Testament interpretation seems to be needed. Such would be developed from both the existing methods of rhetorical criticism used for New Testament interpretation and a meta-theoretical analysis of what a method of rhetorical criticism for New Testament interpretation ought to consist.

2.4.2   Rhetoric as Persuasion

From the review of the rhetorical theory above, a rhetorical theory deemed appropriate for the rhetorical criticism of a New Testament text, in particular, a Pauline epistle, is one in which rhetoric is considered as persuasion, conceptualized as a particular process with particular possible goals. Although generally, rhetoric can be defined as the "deliberate, calculated use of language for the sake of communicating various kinds of information in a manner intended by the speaker (and the theory of such a use),"[51] rhetoric is conceptualized here as the persuasive strategies that serve response-shaping, response-reinforcing, and response-changing purposes. This view of rhetoric is to be distinguished from two other major views of rhetoric that also have long traditions. These are the stylistic view, reducing rhetoric to techniques of ornamentation, and a comprehensive view, which broadens rhetoric into covering all the techniques and rules of textual composition, both spoken and written.[52] Apparently, this broader view encompasses many and various approaches and overlaps considerably with the modern field of textual linguistics.

Persuasion is a process with several key components.[53] Typically, the author is the human originator of the message. The author has a vision, an intended impact that is sought for the reader. The author constructs and conveys a message to the reader through a channel, in this case the biblical text. The author would have a desired outcome to happen to the reader, which we refer to as authorial intended impact. In view of the author's intended impact, the author determines the needed understanding that should inhabit the reader for the reader to reflect or experience the impact the author desires. We refer to this as the authorial meaning. Since

---

51. Classen, *Rhetorical Criticism*, 45.

52. For more insights on these aspects, see Trible *Rhetorical Criticism*; Longman, *Literary Approaches*.

53. For a fuller discussion on this see Mbennah, "Impact of Audience," 54; "Communication," 88.

the author has a desired end result on the reader, and since that end result depends on some particular understanding that the reader should have, it implies that the author has the responsibility to state or decide what the intended impact to be sought is and determine the necessary understanding that the reader needs to have for the intended impact to occur.

As part of the persuasion process there may be reflections back to the author in view of the message and its presentation, referred to as feedback. The reflections may be subtle or overt, voluntary or involuntary, immediate or delayed. Such reflections from the reader may indicate approval or disapproval of what is being communicated, clarity or lack of clarity of what is being communicated, acceptance or rejection of the proposals inherent in the communication, or simply suggest something in relation to the quality of the venue or the state of the reader. But also, often, the reflections will come from the message itself back to the author, for example, if the message is not organized or is not flowing well, or if the level or quality of language is not commensurate with that particular reader. It is also possible that the channel used will send indications to the author that not all is well with the communication event. However, in biblical texts, the feedback element may not be applicable.

In the course of persuasion, any number of factors would interfere with the reader's processing and responding to the message. These factors may come from the very person and specific characteristics of the author, as the reader perceives the quality and nature of the message, the quality and nature of the channel, and the reader itself. These factors are referred to as noise. The audience is the primary target of the persuasion. According to Perelman and Olbrechts-Tyteca (1958), audiences are basically one of two types, particular and universal, but in either case an appeal is made to an audience on the basis of their value system. This value system is based on the experience and the group affiliation of the audience, and the appeal made by the speaker will be based on his understanding of their beliefs and values. The "universal audience" is in fact a creation of the mind of the author, his conception of an audience most reasonable and most competent with respect to the issues under discussion. And, importantly, the author must be a member of the universal audience; because the universal audience is final judge and arbiter of what the author is arguing, and because the author is a part of that audience, the argument itself cannot be manipulative. After the reader—the audience of a written material—reads the text from the author, the reader will develop some meaning, which will result

The Mature Church

in some impact. These are referred to as actual meaning and actual impact, respectively.

A number of implications could be drawn from the foregoing conceptualization of persuasion. First, an attempt to communicate persuasively implies the presence of an intended effect and the appropriate steps to reach that effect. Second, as a purposeful enterprise, persuasion attempts to modify some targeted beliefs, values or behaviors of the target readers to some predetermined new state. It therefore seems that the author would preselect and execute appropriate rhetorical strategies through which the reader is guided to interpret and respond to the author's propositions in a manner as closely congruent to the intentions of the author as possible.

Third, authorial intentionality is assumed or implied, also in terms of the impact, meaning, text organization, and general rhetorical strategies employed. Intentionality is also assumed in terms of creation or generation of meaning, in which regard two matters ought to be noted. The one is that the creation of meaning is a dual process involving the communication author and the reader, and the other is how meaning actually mediates the occurrence of communication. As I define elsewhere, "Meaning could be defined as that product of cognitive construction from perceived information cues, which is also influenced by cultural as well as psychological and context-specific pragmatic factors."[54] Thus, whereas the author's intended meaning is a product of a prewriting construction process, the reader's actual meaning is an inference to the cues and symbols transmitted by the author. Presumably, the author would define, albeit intuitively, the necessary meaning that would lead to the desired end result of a particular text, as well as determine and employ the appropriate methods and means to achieve that meaning. The reader will, of his or her own nature, process the incoming stimuli to construct a meaning. I suggest then that the significance of meaning in mediating persuasion is that, because readers have reference frames with which they see the world around them in a stable way, each time new meaning reaches a reader, that meaning contrastively asserts itself over or against the existing frame of reference. Subsequently, the reader behaviorally and/or attitudinally readjusts to the new understanding.

From this understanding of rhetoric as persuasion there are particular possible intended outcomes. Miller identifies three possible behavioral outcomes of persuasion, namely, response shaping, response reinforcing,

---

54. Mbennah, "Impact," 29.

and response changing.⁵⁵ But also being persuaded could refer to response terminating, which can be reducing hostility (defusion) or becoming ambivalent about a former position (neutralizing). Response shaping pertains to cases where the audience does not initially possess a particular pattern of responses to some stimuli. In such cases, being persuaded means obtaining, through a communication, formed and conditioned responses to those stimuli. Thus, response shaping leads to the acquisition of new beliefs or behaviors. This kind of being persuaded could be equated with learning and socialization, and is in fact attitude formation, not attitude change. Response reinforcing refers to intensifying existing convictions, activating them into actions, and deterring the weakening of support. Hence, since people are in the process of being persuaded, response reinforcing always requires to be sustained by multiple messages. Most definitions of persuasion also imply that "being persuaded" is response changing.⁵⁶ Response changing refers to converting others and inducing crystallization of attitudes or behaviors, say, by soliciting single-mindedness from the audience through shading off conflicting attitudes.

Miller's response-reinforcing process is most often exemplified in sermons and political speeches, where the aim is to reinforce currently held convictions so as to make them more resistant to change. This category is seen here as useful for defining religious-ethical exhortatory discourse or paraenesis as a subcategory of the conative function so as to be distinguished from response-changing process most commonly regarded as the essential characteristic of persuasion.

As a purposeful enterprise, rhetoric then attempts to modify some targeted beliefs or behaviors of the audience to some predetermined new state. Persuasion therefore refers to that effect upon the audience—attitudinal or behavioral or both—that the author seeks to achieve through forming and presenting appropriate arguments, adapting them to the specific audience.

2.4.3 Rhetorical Dimensions of the First Readers

The classical rhetorical legacy, in particular the reforms carried out by Cicero and Quintilian, as discussed earlier, meant that there were rhetorical forms, systems, or traditions that characterized the socio-cultural context

---

55. Miller, "On Being Persuaded," 17.
56. See for example Brembeck and Howell, *Persuasion*; Scheidel *Persuasive Speaking*; Cronkhite, *Persuasion*.

The Mature Church

within which the New Testament texts were written and compiled. This implies that understanding and interpreting such a text requires at least both an appreciation of the rhetorical tradition of the first readers and an understanding as well as application of the principles of rhetorical interpretation that formed part of the context of the first readers. From this viewpoint, the meaning of a New Testament text is to be determined through the rhetorical forms that the writer would have used, what rhetorical objectives the author would have had, and how the original recipients would have interpreted the message. Furthermore, because both the recipients and the speakers lived in a socio-linguistic world shaped by the conscious rhetoric of Hellenism, the preachers' desires to provoke a response were incarnated in Hellenistic rhetoric, as Pogoloff well puts it:

> As part of a self-conscious rhetorical culture, the New Testament texts implicitly and often explicitly partake of the recognition that human realities occur in linguistic worlds. Just as philosophy could not escape the dominance of rhetoric, neither could the writers of the New Testament. Christian proclamation is thus subsumed in rhetoric. It strives not to establish itself vis-à-vis rational or empirical knowledge, but to discover and shape a linguistic world while simultaneously seeking to transcend that world. Its point of departure is not epistemology, but rhetoric.[57]

On the other hand, Cameron for example, points out that Christian discourse in the Roman world both made its impact on the society at large and was itself transformed and shaped in the endeavor, so much so that Christian discourse would have been different without the environment of the Roman world. Cameron contends that, for Christian discourse, there were a series of overlapping discourses always in a state of adaptation and adjustment, and always ready to absorb in a highly opportunistic manner whatever might be useful from secular rhetoric and vocabulary.[58] Hence, ultimately, an evolution of an organized system of thought led, so to speak, to a language of Christian faith, with its own themes and forms of expressing those themes. This implies that the early church became a distinct rhetorical community.

If the New Testament is to be seen as (persuasive) communication, it means that the first recipients of the texts of the New Testament would be seen as audiences. This calls for discussion of the essential nature of

---

57. Pogoloff, "Isocrates," 351.
58. See Cameron, *Christianity*.

audiences and incorporation of the same in building up a method of rhetorical criticism. Symbolic convergence theory posits that through interaction people converge into entities, defined in that respect by shared rhetorical visions and bound into rhetorical communities.[59]

Basic to the symbolic convergence theory is the view that reality is socially construed and socially based. Because people in the same group share inputs and interpretations from the environment, they come to hold those inputs and interpretations more strongly than if they had experienced them separately. People have fantasies, those "creative and imaginative interpretations of events that fulfil a psychological or rhetorical need."[60] When the sharing of fantasy occurs fully there is a symbolic convergence of the meaning, which comes as a result of a "unified putting together of the various scripts which gives the participant a broader view of things."[61] Audiences, therefore, are entities that have created and share specific messages that contain reality, reality that differs from the mere existence of phenomena.

One of the assumptions upon which symbolic convergence theory is based is that symbols not only create reality for individuals, but individuals' meanings for symbols can converge to create shared reality for participants. "Convergence" in the theory refers to the way two or more private symbolic worlds incline towards each other, come more closely together, or even overlap during certain processes of communication. Such convergence results in a number of consequences: individuals may jointly experience the same emotions; they may develop the same attitudes and emotional responses to the *personae* of the drama, or may interpret some aspect of their experience in the same way.

What symbolic convergence theory implies is that different audiences have their own rhetorical visions and constitute rhetorical communities along with corresponding symbolic systems. The basic unit of symbolic convergence theory and fantasy-theme criticism is fantasy or fantasy theme. In this case, fantasy is the creative and imaginative interpretation of events, and fantasy theme is the means through which the interpretation is accomplished. Rhetorical vision is also an important concept in symbolic convergence theory and in the fantasy-theme approach. As Bormann defines it, rhetorical vision is a "unified putting together of the various shared fantasies" or a swirling together of fantasy themes to provide a credible

59. See Bormann's "Fantasy" and "Symbolic Convergence Theory."
60. Bormann, "Symbolic Convergence Theory," 130.
61. Bormann, *Force of Fantasy*, 8.

35

interpretation of reality.[62] The presence of a rhetorical vision suggests that a rhetorical community has been formed consisting of participants in the vision or members who share fantasy themes.

Thus, we would propose that the first readers of New Testament texts constituted and belonged to communities—that is, sets of people who shared the same meanings for basic values. Pogoloff agrees that there could be understanding of the rhetoric of the early Christians when it is read within the communicative conventions of that age, but argues that when we enter the rhetorical world of Hellenistic society we discover not only communicative conventions, but a worldview in which speech was valued, used, and understood in ways that profoundly affected the proclamation and understanding of the gospel.[63]

Also, since the New Testament writers were conscious of the fact that they had been entrusted with a revelation and a commission to witness to that revelation[64] and, consequently, saw their speech as prophetic, it means that their rhetorical situation differed from that of the civic orators. But their rhetorical situation also differed from that of the prophets in that their preaching became directed primarily toward non-Jews rather than Jews, which meant that the proclamation aimed to provoke conversion before faithfulness.

Furthermore, since audience expectations shape rhetoric and there are rhetorical effects of identification,[65] the change in the audience from Jewish to Gentile could have "forced" the New Testament writers to change language worlds. But incarnating the Christian message in the language of non-Christian culture is fraught with danger, since content and form always coinhere. This problem can be read in 1 Corinthians, where the Apostle Paul employs words common in non-Christian use, such as σωφια and λογος. But the discourse of 1 Corinthians forces the reader to interpret these words in senses unfamiliar to Hellenistic culture. Never could the Corinthians, without the intrusion of Paul's discourse, imagine how wisdom—for them the highest achievement of culture—could be weak and foolish, nor how weakness and foolishness (what is culturally despised) could be wise. Paul begins with the community sense and then deforms it, using words that originally implied power and syntactically relating them to the weakness of the cross.

---

62. Ibid.
63. Pogoloff, "Isocrates and Contemporary Hermeneutics," 339.
64. Cf. 1 John 1:3; Gal 1:11; Mark 10:20; Acts 6:7; 19:20, 1 Cor 2:13; 1 Thess 2:13.
65. See Burke, *Rhetoric of Motives*, 55.

So, in one sense, the first Christian preachers, like other orators, would communicate only insofar as they could speak within the previously established world of the audience. But if they stopped there, they would have been no more than another group of civic orators. Instead, they claimed that human words in their rhetoric was only the beginning, not the end (cf. 1 Thess 2:13).

Once formed, communities frequently maintain their communal language, worldview, and identity by means of a canon of approved texts, hence New Testament texts could be understood within the framework of a communal world maintained within tradition, canon, and authority. This in turn means that the New Testament texts would have recorded the rhetoric of particular situations, rhetoric that aimed to draw the original readers deeper into realities that both intersected and transcended their everyday experience. According to Stowers, "aside from a purely religious thought, Jewish traditions made a permanent impress on Christian letters in the use of the Old Testament language, prayers, thanksgivings, and blessings. Paul, the Hellenistic Jew, provided the most important models for Christian letters."[66] Christians thought of themselves as a third race, neither Jewish nor Greek, and this meant that they were to form their own self-governing communities, marking their own celebrations and writing their own literature. This desire for self-definition was so strong and persisted for so long that during the first three centuries there were produced several brands of Christianity. Many early Christian groups developed a character-building desire, with notable complex hortatory or paranaetic letters. Paul knows and uses the terms for and techniques of different kinds of exhortation, often aiming to building the character of Christian communities, rather than individuals. Individuals are exhorted to have virtues and dispositions that contribute to the development and quality of life of the community. Paul attributes the community life to the power and work of God, thereby departing from the classical notion of friendship. There was thus emerging a peculiar audience, not only in the content of letters but also in the organization and emphasis of that content.

---

66. Stowers, *Letter Writing*, 41.

2.4.4 Rhetorical Dimensions of the Text

A number of scholars[67] recognize that the model for Paul's letters is to be found in the Greek letter writing tradition.[68] It is possible to identify the letter structure and the parts of a speech and then argue that the elements of the letter structure and the formulae that are associated with them are a harmonious part of the rhetoric of the letter. From epistolary theory, the letter was situational and assumed that the recipient would do something as a result of having received it. Understood rhetorically, a letter did not just convey information but, even when its purpose was as simple as maintaining contact, prompted decisions to be made. Furthermore, since epistles were occasioned by some particular circumstances,[69] it implies that there is in each text of an epistle, for example, a goal, an outcome, or an impact on the reader desired by the author, constituting, implicitly or explicitly, a particular outcome or an authorial intended outcome as a rhetorical dimension of the text.

Another rhetorical dimension of the text is the apparent authorial intended meaning. A message is that set of symbols packaged and delivered in a manner so as to generate in the reader a meaning that would most likely lead to a particular authorial intended impact on the reader.

To sum up this section, the rhetorical dimensions of the text are structure, argumentation, apparent authorial intended goal or outcome, apparent authorial intended impact, and the general potential of the text to generate an impact defined by the author. Stowers' discussion shows that many of the Pauline letters focused on family ethos, viewing the church as a family, and focus on exhortation, appraising Paul as the bold but gentle teacher and censuring false teachers. The hortatory letters are akin to deliberative rhetoric, in which action is sought or required of the readers. Thus, from the various types of Ancient Greco-Roman letters,[70] many of the Christian letters, especially the Pauline epistles, became increasingly hortatory and exhortational and admonishing in nature.

---

67. See for example Classen, *Rhetorical Criticism*, 1–44.

68. For extended discussions on ancient letter writing, see Aune, *New Testament*, 158ff.; Stowers, *Letter Writing*, 27–35, 58–173; Stowers, "Social Typification," 78ff.

69. See Fee & Stuart, *How to Read*, 45.

70. For a good discussion of these see Stowers, *Letter Writing*, 58–173.

2.4.5 Rhetorical Dimensions of the Author

There is no doubt that by the time the writers produced the text of the New Testament, in particular the Apostle Paul, the legacies of Plato and Aristotle as well as that of other earlier rhetoricians would have been highly pronounced. There would have been, for example, a well-established rhetoric of letters, which would have had the forms of writing found in the epistles. Also, both the Jewish religious expressions and Hellenistic piety were part of the world that shaped the New Testament text, and from Cicero's view of rhetoric as a system of general culture, men were being trained to write and speak competently in all subjects. Similarly, an extensive educational reform by Quintilian, whose life would have overlapped much of the lives of many of the New Testament writers, may have boosted the study of rhetoric. As he wrote or preached, Paul would have done so within and from his Hellenistic as well as Greco-Roman and Jewish contexts.[71]

It would therefore be incorrect to insist that Paul's letters are a different type from those listed in the ancient handbooks. After all, the handbooks simply provided examples of how letter writers might respond to a variety of situations that could be addressed by means of a letter. Paul paid attention to formal conventions and topics associated with letters and did not hesitate to modify those conventions to serve the purpose of his argument. However, it is clear, and a source of continuing frustration for scholars, that his letters are not like others, whether from the tradition of literary letters, official correspondence, or private letters. They cannot be neatly categorized.

Structurally, Paul's letters are more complex, with at least four major sections found in most: the opening greeting, which typically uses χάρις as a substitute for χαίρειν and as a substitute for the health wish; the thanksgiving period; the body, a section of teachings or moral exhortations; and the closing greeting. The opening greeting can be extensively elaborate (e.g., Rom 1:1–7) and could even mention his office or role in the life of his mission, i.e., a slave of Christ for the benefit of those to whom he writes. It

---

71. Paul would have used a secretary in some fashion, as that was a common practice in the Greco-Roman literary life of Paul's day (see Richards, *Paul*, 81–91); he even used some of the terminology of the ancient Greek rhetoric, and may have used the notion of the household code not without an association of his knowledge of the household codes that existed during his time, even he may have modified the specific content of the codes. Classen (*Rhetorical Criticism*, 45ff.) presents a "rhetorical reading" of the Epistle to Titus, a Pauline epistle, to demonstrate that Paul often utilized contemporary rhetorical theory in writing the epistles.

concludes not with a conventional word of greeting but with kind of benedictory declaration of grace that supplants the health wish. In five of the seven undisputed Pauline letters Paul includes the names of others as sending the letter. The greeting is followed by a thanksgiving period that usually contains reference to the topics that will be elaborated upon in the body. The body is designed to do more than maintain friendly relations, make a request, seek information, or give an order. His letters often seek to do all these things and more. The body can have three parts to it, with opening, transitional, and closing formulae marking the trajectory of the development of the message. What this means is that although Paul paid attention to formal conventions and topics associated with letters, he sometimes modified those conventions and topics to suit the purpose of his argument.

Furthermore, since the epistle is not primarily paraenetic in function, Paul follows the body of the letter with a section of moral exhortations or instructions. An examination of any of the epistles written by the Apostle Paul would suggest that the closing greeting is often extensively elaborated and usually serves as a kind of epilogue. Paul tends to ignore or adapt standard conventions and uses instead benedictions, greetings to various people, a personal signature, doxology, exhortations and recommendations, or some combination of these. The function of the letter as representing the writer's presence is given high prominence by the probability that the letter carrier was Paul's emissary and played an important role in its presentation to the audience.

Thus, the Apostle Paul would have had his own inventional strategy. For example, he used irony as a rhetorical technique in his correspondence with the church at Corinth. Keeping in mind that the primary purpose of private letters was to maintain friendly contact over distance, it is evident that when Paul was confronted with one or more exigencies involving one of the churches he had helped start, he would turn to the letter as the medium of communication. It is also apparent from his letters that he needed to do more than fulfill the conventional purposes for which letters were used. Given the audience and rhetorical situation, it seems likely he would turn to conventions and topics associated with Greco-Roman rhetoric to help him in the process of addressing the exigency, so he could use two tools available to him, namely, epistolary theory and rhetorical theory.

But Paul would have faced some significant constraints. Whereas epistolary theory advocated careful wording and clarity of style in order to avoid misunderstanding that could arise when one could not see one's audience,[72] and private letters rarely attempted to deal with more than one topic,[73] in most cases, as the epistles generally reflect, Paul had to deal with more than one exigency and thus needed to elaborate on more than one topic in a given letter. The multiplicity of audiences in the Pauline letters meant that the argumentative situation in any one letter became more complex. No doubt Paul had to imagine the effect of his argument on both the particular audience and the universal audience and then make appropriate adjustments in its course. Thus, for example, Paul may have had to use enthymematic reasoning in one section of the argument, making it appear to be more forensic-like; or argument from example in another, and thus make it appear more deliberative. Similarly, I would suppose, he would have selected topics from the genre of Greco-Roman speech, or from rabbinic argumentation, or even from arguments becoming common in the emerging Christian argumentation system.

Furthermore, it could also be suggested that a given rhetorical situation could be made complex by the audience setting. For the Galatians, for example, one letter had to be addressed to audiences whose physical location and, most probably, spiritual understandings, were different. In contrast, Paul's Epistle to Philemon—whose purpose could be categorized as maintaining friendly contact and whose topic can be described as an appeal for "family" members to be reconciled—has a public tone to it and may have been intended to be read to the church meeting in Philemon's house. Also, it seems that the Apostle Paul was conscious of his need to persuade a particular audience by appeal to the values of universal audience and by his membership in that audience.

Because issues of character are important exigencies in so many of the undisputed letters, the establishment of his ethos often takes precedence as a mode of persuasion even in letters to those he knows well, and the topics of honour and shame, or blame and praise, are quite common.

Thus, to sum up this section, the Apostle Paul may have had a particular style, consisting of generally following, but also often deviating from,

---

72. The theory of epistolary types required, for example, that the writer compose according to generic patterns, which had to fit the circumstances of the author's particular situation in writing. The "particular situation" would include the author's relationship with the audience, the prevailing state of that relationship, and what occasioned the writing of the letter (see Stowers, *Letter Writing*, 53).

73. See the examples of the letters as the ancient letter writing handbooks taught in Stowers, *Letter Writing*, 58ff.), although the letter types provided rather bare outlines, with room for the writer to adapt.

the letter writing conventions of that time: particular argumentation style, cognizance of multiplicity of audience segments within larger audiences, consciousness of and distinction between particular and universal audiences, his personal identification with the audience, and establishing ethos.

2.5 Summary

Rhetorical criticism, I propose, should be seen as an approach utilizing various possible rhetorical methods. An exegete would need to build up a method of rhetorical criticism for each specific purpose, depending on the type of New Testament text with which the exegete is dealing. One has to come to terms with the fact that just what sort of interpretational end result one would achieve, would depend on the specific rhetorical critical method one develops—whether, for example, it is the meaning as intended by the author and hence by the Holy Spirit, the impact upon the first audience of that meaning, or the specific style of the human source of that text.

I propose that each New Testament text is to be viewed as communication, and this means that interpretation of that text necessarily needs a consideration of the early church as a distinct rhetorical community. As such, the rhetorical conventions of the first-century Christians, as a community of believers, would need to be constructed. These rhetorical conventions should form a specific kind of socio-historic context of the human source of the text and the original audience. It thus calls for, on the one hand, a consideration of the general context of the time of the occasion as well as the time of its recording, and, on the other hand, construction of the specific context of the first audience as a rhetorical community with its own view of sacred truth and forms of expressing that sacred truth as well as their reaction toward "secular" forms of communication.

It is in this regard that I also propose that one should see the writings of the New Testament, therefore also Ephesians, as a unique type of discourse that would have commanded a particular view by the early Christians. One should then try to understand the rhetorical devices the rhetoricians would have employed in the process and their corresponding purposes as well as what would have been the expected response of the audience, and on that basis understand the meaning. The meaning would have been tied to the objective, which would have been tied to the exigency.

Therefore, a method of rhetorical criticism for interpreting Ephesians 4:13, or indeed any Pauline epistle passage, would require the following:

- **Determine the rhetorical context:** determine and describe the rhetorical situation, and identify the dimensions of authorial purpose, author, message, channel, primary audience, and social and specific audience contexts.
- **Determine the rhetorical dimensions of the author:** ethos, explicit and implicit invitation of the author for the audience to consider the claims, the rhetorical authority, rhetorical objective, and rhetorical strategies.
- **Determine the rhetorical dimensions of the first recipients:** the emotional, the socio-cultural, rhetorical conventions, socio-historic context, and possible intended response.
- **Determine the rhetorical dimensions of the text:** rhetorical force, intended meaning, rhetorical potential, invitation of the text for the audience to consider the claims therein, claims or arguments in the text and the grounds of those claims, imposing nature of the claims over the rhetorical conventions of the recipients, and potency of the text to invite desired impact.
- **Deduce authorial meaning and intended impact:** specific audience aspirations stated or implied, specific change called for or implied, and intended meaning and intended impact (scope, dimensions, sustainability, evidence, necessity, benefits, consequences).

3

Communicative Function of Ephesians 4:1–16

3.1 Introduction

EPHESIANS 4:1–16 HAS A particular communicative function within the general rhetorical structure of the epistle. The Epistle to the Ephesians has three[1] primary and distinctive parts: chapters 1–3, presenting a theological treatise; 4:17–6:20, presenting the practical side of the Christian life; and the pericope 4:1–16, presenting the bridge between the two parts, not only in the sense of being at the middle of the two parts but especially in the sense of being the mechanism by which the practical life in 4:17—6:20 is made possible in light of the doctrine of 1:3—3:20. In this chapter I elucidate these aspects and discuss them, with a view to establishing a basis for the interpretation of 4:13. First, by way of argument, an attempt is made to

---

1. The majority of introductions and commentaries on the epistle consider it to have two parts, namely, 1:1—3:21 and 4:1—6:22. Lincoln (*Ephesians*), for example, says the letter has two distinctive but related parts and points out that recognition of these two parts is determinative for discussion of each area in terms of content, structure, genre, and style. Similarly, Stott (Message, 15) describes the epistle as a comprehensive sum¬mary of the good news, on the one hand, and the implications of the good news, on the other; that the Epistle would move the reader to wonder and worship, on the one hand, and challenge the reader to consistency of life, on the other. In his exposition, Stott presents four main sections of the epistle: new life (1:3—2:10), new society (2:11—3:21); new standards (4:1—5:20), and new relationships (5:21—6:24); but clearly, for him, the first two represent the good news, and the remaining two sections the implications of the good news. O'Brien (*Epistle*) also treats the epistle from the view that the primary parts of the epistle are 1:3—3:21, a doctrinal part the essence of which is the divine creation of a new humanity, and 4:1—6:20, a paraenetic part essentially presenting the earthly life of the new humanity. Guthrie (*Pauline Epistles*, 136ff.), though he subdivides the first part, after the salutation, into three subparts, also reflects two primary parts of the Epistle.

establish the rhetoricity[2] of the epistle, after which an examination of the rhetorical structure of Ephesians is done, in order to establish the rhetorical purpose of Ephesians and the function of 4:1–16 in the epistle. From the analysis of the structure of the epistle, the relationship between the three sections is also determined.

3.2 Rhetoricity of the Epistle to the Ephesians

To delineate the communicative function of Ephesians 4:1–16 requires, among other things, establishing the rhetoricity of the epistle, which in turn requires an examination of the elements of the rhetorical process, that is, the author, the recipients, the structure, and the arguments of the epistle.

3.2.1 The Rhetorical Dimensions of the Author

To do a rhetorical-critical analysis of a biblical text, it may be necessary to know the author of the particular text,[3] depending on the method of rhetorical criticism one chooses to use. Although a rhetorical process per se could proceed without necessarily having conclusive opinion about or knowledge of the author, without a definite view on authorship the rhetorical critic does not have a contextual reference point to determine meaning and authorial intent. This is because the determination of the author becomes necessary for the temporal location of the text, which is needed to determine the significance of the word symbols and other communicative devices used in the text. That is to say, resolving the issue of authorship provides a necessary basis to understand the historical context of the text. Therefore, a decision has to be made on the authorship of Ephesians. An entire Pauline authorship would mean it was wholly written by the Apostle Paul, sent to one or more communities from which he was separated. If so,

---

2. The term "rhetoricity" is used here to refer to the question whether Ephesians is a rhetorical document, presenting an argument and possessing a structure and, therefore, lending itself to a valid process of rhetorical criticism.

3. In general, the authority of a biblical text is not dependent upon the human author. However, in rhetorical criticism, one recognizes that the perceived human source of the arguments influences the audience's reception, processing and responding to the arguments or appeals of the text. It is therefore of interest to the rhetorical critic to identify the relationship between the (human) author and the recipients. And, more, knowing the author in terms of who he was and what his views were could be critical in understanding the broader context of the epistle.

the epistle would have to be fitted into a plausible biography and socio-historical setting of Paul's career. If, on the other hand, it is a *pseudepigraphon*,[4] it will be necessary to guess its social and historical setting. If this were true it would even be incorrect to describe Ephesians as a letter, because it will mean that although it is in letter form, it was never sent anywhere; it only "emerged" and its "readers" were not its recipients as such.

The majority of post-nineteenth-century scholars reject the traditional view of the Pauline authorship of Ephesians.[5] But the arguments against Pauline authorship are inconclusive.[6] In particular, the different aspects of style, such as the apparent reflective mode and slower pace, are not a sufficient basis to reject the Pauline authorship of Ephesians. It is not inconceivable that Paul would choose another style, in view of a different context of writing or of the recipients. On the other hand, a Paulinist imitator, had there been one, would have produced a more stilted summary of Paul's doctrines and themes, which is not the case.[7]

---

4. A pseudepigraphon is a document that claims to have been written by someone other than its real author (Muddiman, *Commentary*, 2). This is to be distinguished from anonymous authors, whereby the author is simply not known and the work is attributed to an appropriate authority (See O'Brien, *Epistle*, 37).

5. Lincoln (*Ephesians*, lx), for example, presupposes authorship of Ephesians by a follower of Paul. He identifies the characteristics, views, and concerns of the implied author intrinsic in the text and therefrom proposes Paul, a secretary, or a later follower as the possible actual authors. He quickly dismisses Paul and the secretary, saying it simply could not be Paul and the secretary hypothesis would not solve problem of changes in theology. Apparently, Lincoln has undergone a change of view, away from a Pauline authorship he held previously, arguing that to see the letter as the work of a later follower of Paul makes better sense of its contents. He says that although the implied author is the Apostle Paul, the actual author was a later follower, who employed the literary device of pseudonymity. Best (*Critical and Exegetical*, 14) too favors non-Pauline authorship and goes on to defend pseudonymous writing as having been common, even among first-century Christians. Muddiman (*Commentary*, 21–23) takes a middle ground, between authenticity and pseudepigraphy. His position is that Ephesians contains within it a genuine letter of Paul, originally written to the Laodiceans, which was edited and expanded by a later follower, and actually goes ahead to reconstruct Paul's letter to the Laodiceans (ibid., 302, 303).

6. These views include the close relationship with Colossians in terms of structure and language style, from which a dependence theory on the part of Ephesians has been proposed (see Lincoln, *Ephesians*, lxviii). But Guthrie (*Pauline Epistles*, 114) says the use of the same words and phraseology in different senses would be only difficult when used within a very short time interval between the two epistles, and only if the differences in usage are incompatible in one mind and are apparently inconceivable for the works of the writer to whom they are attributed; but this is not the case here.

7. Guthrie's position (*Pauline Epistles*, 127,128) is worthy noting: "When all the

Those who doubt or reject the Pauline authorship of the epistle also note that when addressing himself to any particular church, even where he had not been, the Apostle always assumes a personal tone (for example, in Thessalonians, Galatians, and Corinthians). In their view, since in Ephesians he is not as characteristically personal—at least not personal enough with his correspondents[8]—he may not be the author of Ephesians. This argument leads to the conclusion that either it was not the Apostle Paul who wrote Ephesians, or, if he did, he did not address it to the church at Ephesus.[9] In agreeing with the Pauline authorship of Ephesians, on account of lack of a particularly personal flavor, one view is that the epistle is to be considered a circular letter[10] to a group of churches hitherto still largely unknown to Paul. But this explanation, founded on the encyclical character of the epistle, loses its value if the church of Ephesus is numbered among those addressed, since during his three-year sojourn in this city the Apostle would have had frequent intercourse with the neighboring Christian communities, and in this case he would have had Ephesus especially in view.

However, when the fullest consideration is given to the basic facts, the Pauline authorship of the Ephesians is sustained. First, the Epistle claims to be the work of Paul both directly (1:1, 3:1) and indirectly (4:1, 6:20,21). Second, there is ample evidence of universal acceptance of it as Paul's from

---

objections are carefully considered it will be seen that the weight of evidence is inadequate to overthrow the overwhelming external attestation to Pauline authorship, and the Epistle's own claims. . . . To maintain that the Paulinist out of his sheer love for Paul and through his own self-effacement composed the letter, attributed it to Paul and found an astonishing and immediate readiness on the part of the church to recognize it as such is considerably less credible than the simple alternative of regarding it as Paul's own work."

8. The claim that the epistle has impersonal tone uncharacteristic of the Apostle Paul is untenable because the apostle is not any less personal with the Ephesians than he is with recipients in his undisputed letters. Yes, Paul does send extended personal greetings in 1 & 2 Corinthians, Galatians, and Philippians—churches he knew well. But he is personally involved with the Ephesians also, sharing extended personal information (3:1-4), praying for them (1:15-23; 3:14-21), requesting their prayers (6:18-20), and sending Tychicus to tell them more personal information about him (6:21).

9. It is known that Paul spent about three years at Ephesus and planted the church there, so he would not write in a manner to suggest that he does not personally know the Ephesians.

10. Guthrie (*Pauline Epistles*, 130ff.) presents and discusses several other theories on the destination of the epistle. Although he is not definitive on one, he seems to favor the circular letter theory.

ancient until modern times.¹¹ Third, there is sufficient internal evidence to the effect that Paul is its author.¹²

I therefore conclude and hold the view that Paul the Apostle is indeed the author of the epistle designated as Ephesians. This is Paul, a Jew by birth, born in the first decade AD in Tarsus, a small prosperous city on the trade route from Syria to Asia Minor.¹³ He would have obtained his education both in the Greek disciplines of rhetoric and classical literature and in the pharisaic approach to Jewish Law under the famous Rabbi Gamaliel (Acts 22:3). Paul, hitherto Saul, would have attended Greek schools with Gentiles and learned about God in a Synagogue of Greek-speaking Pharisees. He became an outstanding rabbi and was a member of the Sanhedrin.¹⁴ He became the most ardent anti-Christian leader in Judaism (Acts 22:4–5) who passionately hated Christians. Around AD 35, on his way to Damascus to arrest and persecute Christians, Jesus Christ confronted him and revealed to him that he was persecuting the very God he professed to worship (Acts 9:1–19).

11. Marcion (AD 140) included it in his canon as Pauline, the oldest compilation of the writings of the Apostle. At that stage, Pauline authorship was undisputed, except that Marcion retitled it as "Laodiceans." Similarly, in the Moratorium Canon (AD 180) Ephesians was included under the letters of Paul. Furthermore, it forms part of the Pauline epistles in the earliest evidence for the Latin and Syriac versions and many other ancient manuscripts (see Guthrie, *Pauline Epistles*, 100). Also, Ireneaus cites Eph 5:30 as being from an epistle to the Ephesians, Clement of Alexandria cites Eph 5:21–15 as from the Epistle to the Ephesians, and Tertullian criticizes Marcion for changing the name of the Epistle to the Ephesians to "Laodiceans" (Guthrie, *Pauline Epistles*, 129). Furthermore, O'Brien (*Epistle*, 41) points out that the Epistle to the Laodiceans was clearly a spurious letter that was ascribed to Paul, presumably to fill the vacuum which arose as a result of a lost letter mentioned in Colossians 4:16.

12. There is a wealth of Pauline phraseology contained in Ephesians—there is hardly a line in the whole letter that does not show some resemblance to one or another of the nine undisputed letters of Paul. It is known, for example (see Guthrie, *Pauline Epistles*, 129, 130), that the word "faith" occurs ninety-eight times in those nine letters, or about once per page, which is also the average maintained in Ephesians—eight occurrences in eight pages. Similarly, "justification" occurs forty-nine times in the nine genuine letters, an average of one occurrence of the word every two pages, but three times in Ephesians, or once in two and a half pages, but the "justification" is not found in Colossians. O'Brien (*Epistle*, 45–46) notes that in view of the distinctiveness of Ephesians among the Pauline letters and the high significance of the early and consistent attestation to its Pauline authorship, and because the Christians of the first century were closer to the situation when it was written and were careful in weighing and evaluating their founding documents, the uniform testimony to a Pauline authorship should not be easily dismissed.

13. See Simpson & Bruce, *Epistles*.

14. MacArthur, *Ephesians*, xi.

Intrinsic in the text of the epistle, this implied author bears a number of characteristics, views, concerns, and aspirations. He calls himself Paul (1:1, 3:1) and claims apostolic authority (1:1). That his name is explicit in the epistle implies respect and reverence by the recipients. He is writing from prison, where he is suffering for the sake of Christ and for the sake of the gospel and the recipients (3:1,13; 4:1; 6:19, 20). Even so, he exhorts the recipients not to lose heart because of his present suffering (3:13). He has some knowledge of the recipients as he has heard of their faith and love toward other believers (1:13,15); he expresses his personal thanks to God for them (1:16); and he knows the recipients may have heard of his ministry (3:2). He is a servant (3:7), specially appointed by God and given power to be a missionary to the Gentiles, apparently in ways that others were not. He asks for their prayers for him so that he would continue to proclaim the gospel boldly (6:19–20), and he commends Tychicus to the recipients as his representative who will tell them more personal information about him (6:21–22). He variously identifies himself with the recipients but also considers himself less than the least of the saints (3:8). From his citing of the Old Testament and use of the Old Testament tradition, he reflects a high degree of competence in a variety of exegetical methods from Judaism such as midrash pesher.[15]

Furthermore, from the text of the epistle, the author tells the recipients he has a particular revelation regarding their place as Gentiles in the universal church, and invites them to recognize his special insights into the mystery (3:2–6). His mission as an apostle to bring the church into being is part of God's cosmic purpose, and his suffering mediates salvation and eschatological glory to the Gentiles (3:7–13). Besides his specific ministry, he is among the other holy apostles and prophets as a recipient of the revelation of the mystery (3:5), and he is therefore part of the foundation of the church (2:20). He has an appreciation of the salvation God has provided in Christ and an intense awareness that every part of the Christian existence is a pure gift received through God's initiative (see 1:3–14; 2:1–22). He has a vision of greater spiritual quality for the recipients' lives and he is sure the power of God will cause it to happen (1:15–23; 3:14–21). He sees that the Jews and the Gentiles are already united, through Christ's reconciling work and the church is the new creation, replacing the old, divided order. He sees the need for the unity of the church and the place of various offices established by God in the church in producing maturity and, subsequently,

---

15. See Best, *Critical and Exegetical*, 375.

unity (4:1–16). He affirms the recipients' need for a new way of living and thinking against a background of Gentile ignorance (4:17ff.) and he wants the recipients to lead a distinctive life in the world, full of thanksgiving, love, Spirit-filled fellowship, and constant awareness of the battle against evil powers. He sets an exalted view of marriage. From the quality and style of writing, he appears to be a teacher, and a reflective, meditative, and liturgical person. This description fits a Jewish Christian not unlike the Apostle Paul.

3.2.2 The Rhetorical Dimensions of the Recipients

For a rhetorical-critical study of a biblical text it is important to identify the recipients of that text. Typically, a rhetorical-critical analysis of the text would lead to the determination of the authors' implied or declared purpose of his message or the recipients' response sought as well as the rhetorical strategies employed in pursuit of that purpose. To understand the recipients' response to the rhetorical strategy, it is also important to understand the recipients and to determine the rhetorical situation. From the nature of the recipients in terms of their social, spiritual, and other backgrounds, among other things, it becomes possible to gain insight into the intentions of the author. In this section, an attempt will be made to identify and describe the Ephesians, from the social and historical context as well as from the text of epistle.

From the social and historical point of view, there are divergent views with regard to who the recipients of the epistle were,[16] arising from the different views regarding the destination of the epistle.[17] It may be admissible that the epistle was intended for a rather restricted circle of Christian communities, as Tychicus was to visit them all and bring news of him (Eph

---

16. The primary basis for doubting the Ephesian destination is the fact that in the oldest manuscripts, that is, the P4 and in the original hand of the *Vaticanus* and *Sinaiticus*, the words ἐν Ἐφέσῳ are omitted. However, it is better to assume that the reading ἐν Ἐφέσῳ in 1:1 is original; after all, these words are found in the bulk of the witnesses, including *Codex Alexandrianus*.

17. Muddiman's (*Commentary*, 24) view is that a shorter letter was sent to Laodicea (but later expanded by a Paulinist). Betraying his bias for a Laodicean destination, he says "we can further deduce from Col 4:16 that Laodiceans would have been such a usefully to complement Colossians when the letters were exchanged." Obviously his position is influenced by his acceptance of the view that the copy of the letter Marcion had, which lacked reference to the location of the recipients, was addressed to the Laodiceans and that it became the source of Ephesians.

The Mature Church

4:21ff.), which fact precludes the idea of all the churches of Asia Minor or of all the Gentile-Christian churches. On one hand, since Tychicus was the bearer of the Epistle to the Colossians and that to the Ephesians at one and the same time (Col 4:7ff.), those to whom Ephesians was addressed would not have been far from Colossae, thus, with all probability, all of them were in Asia Minor. On the other hand, it is unlikely that Ephesians was addressed to the churches immediately surrounding Colossae, as the trying circumstances that threatened the faith of the Colossians would also endanger that of the neighboring communities as well, and therefore, the two letters would not have been that different in tone and object. Also, having had no personal intercourse with the Colossians, Paul would have been satisfied to address to them and their Christian neighbors one encyclical letter embodying all the matter treated in both epistles. Thus, the addressees of Ephesians must have been different and significantly far from Colossae, though still within Asia Minor.

Even if it were true, as some scholars suggest, that some sections of the epistle seem to imply that Paul did not know the recipients well,[18] a reconstruction of the recipients could be done from the text quite clearly. According to the text, the recipients are "the holy ones who are at Ephesus,[19] the believers who are in Christ Jesus" (1:1).[20] The fact that the epistle was written in Greek implies that most of them understood Greek. Also, they would have been baptized, as 4:5 and 5:26 imply. It appears they have been Christians long enough to know and accept the Old Testament as an authoritative guide of conduct, as it is explicitly quoted or alluded to (Isa 57:19 in 2:12–17, and Ps 68:18 in 4:8). From 2:1ff.; 3:1; and 4:17 it is clear

---

18. Best (*Critical and Exegetical*, 2–3) asserts that non-Christians of the ancient world would not have accepted Paul's high-colored description of the secular world (4:17–19). But it is quite difficult to find a valid basis for this view, given the Paganism of Asia Minor of that time (cf. description of Ephesus of that time by Simpson and Bruce, *Epistles*). This description would exclude non-Jewish readers who were God-fearers.

19. It is likely that "Ephesus" implies a number of Christian communities within Asia Minor, including Ephesus, but not Ephesus alone. But it is possible that the letter was sent to Christians in general, in restricted areas in Asia Minor, as suggested by the lack of any personal greetings and describing the addressees as vaguely as the "saints and faithful." The information in the epistle is not sufficient to allow a conclusive final identification of the recipients and their geographical location with greater precision (see Best *Critical and Exegetical*, 2).

20. Heil (*Ephesians*, 6) points out that although the words "in Ephesus" are not found in some important early manuscripts, there is sufficient text-critical evidence that the recipients were located in Ephesus.

that the majority of the recipients probably were Gentile Christians. The household code in Ephesians (5:21—6:9) may suggest an intended reading by a wider audience than a single congregation in the city of Ephesus, possibly including the churches around the metropolis.[21] Bearing Ephesus as the destination of the epistle makes it difficult to pinpoint a specific Ephesian locale, as Ephesus was a large city,[22] with a significant influence of the social and historical environment upon the recipients. Therefore, the primary destination and implied recipients of the epistle would have been the various local churches within the immediate vicinity of Ephesus.[23]

The epistle is characterized by a "you" and "we" distinction, and a "then" and "now" notion. The "we" would include primarily Christians of Jewish origin, but it would also include early Gentile believers like Titus. Similarly, the "you" would comprise primarily recent converts of Gentile origin, but it also would include Jews in the Diaspora in a Gentile environment who, for not being circumcized, would be considered Gentile. The "you" then would include Gentile converts, former Gentile proselytes, and

---

21. Best (*Critical and Exegetical*, 2 and elsewhere) argues on account of the household code that it reflects on Paul's ignorance or limited knowledge about the recipients, because it supposedly addresses the groups living in wholly Christian families. While it is correct, as Best says, that it is extremely difficult to believe that there was then a Christian community in which every member of every household was a believer, there is no basis in the household code to think that it assumes every member in every family was a Christian.

22. According to Arnold (*Ephesians*, 6), the population of Metropolis Ephesus at this time was at least 250,000 people, and it is possible churches also existed in the villages surrounding Metropolis Ephesus, for example, in the Cayster Valley.

23. According to Simpson and Bruce (*Epistles*), the city of Ephesus, capital of Asia Minor, was the metropolis of a large and populous region, with many nationalities, including Jews and Gentiles. In the first century AD, Ephesus was a place of wealth and luxury, boasting an impressive architecture, especially the Temple of Artemis, one of the Seven Wonders of the Ancient World. Ephesus was also proud of the largest of all Hellenic open-air theatres, capable of holding 50,000 spectators. In the vicinity of this spacious arena lay a stadium for races and wild-beast fights, to which Paul makes allusion in 1 Corinthians, probably using a metaphorical figure of speech. There was rampant idolatry in Ephesus, with Artemis as the goddess of fertility and patroness of propagation. There was widespread fanaticism and superstitions around this laying wonder of image supposedly fallen from heaven. Much abomination of every kind thrived, and much sorcery. The church at Ephesus later on was assailed by false apostles but preserved its integrity, although it lost its vibrancy and enthusiasm. Until the second century AD the church continued to bear a good name.

"God-fearers" who frequented Jewish synagogues as well as Diaspora Jews, but also all those who had become believers recently.[24]

3.2.3 The Rhetorical Purpose in Ephesians

The rhetorical situation has to do with the purpose for writing a rhetorical piece. It has to do with the rhetorical occasion to which a text is understood as a fitting response and the rhetorical problem or problems that the author has to overcome in order to win the recipients over to his point of view. Investigation into a rhetorical situation is to focus on the historical life setting of the recipients and the picture of both the implied author and the recipients that emerges from the text and the rhetorical genre of the text and its strategies. An investigation of the communicative function of the text, determining the desired responses called for as implied by the text, can suggest or imply authorial purpose.[25] The rhetorical situation is critical in a rhetorical-critical process as the message is interpreted through the situation in which it is given. A rhetorical piece can be defined as a communication enterprise so strategically constructed and presented as to achieve an ultimate goal the author desires to see happen in the experience of the recipients. Thus if, as I propose, Ephesians is a rhetorical piece, it means that it has an identifiable ultimate goal or recipient response that Paul desires to achieve and what could be called a strategic construction that would achieve that ultimate goal. It would be possible to also identify that strategic construction.

A survey of literature shows that there is a wide scope of theories of the purpose of Ephesians proposed by various interpreters. There are those interpreters who hold the view that Ephesians does not have any particular purpose[26] or that the purpose cannot be known with certainty.[27] Some

---

24. See Heil, *Ephesians*, 9.

25. For Lincoln (*Ephesians*, lxxv), the mixture of two rhetorical genres in Ephesians—epideictic in the first half, and deliberative in the second—reflects the author's twofold strategy: to intensify the recipients' adherence to Christian convictions, values, and concepts, and to persuade them to take action that will bring their lives to greater conformity with their shared perspective. The first part reinforces their Christian identity, privileges, and status as believers and as part of the church. The second is to appeal to them to demonstrate that identity as they live in the church and in the world.

26. For example, Muddiman (*Commentary*, 14–17) who goes on to compile a survey of recent proposals of the purpose of Ephesians, and then discounts them.

27. See for example Jeal, "Rhetorical Argumentation," 312.

interpreters[28] propose that Ephesians was written to serve as a preface of a collection of Pauline epistles. This proposition is, however, invalid as there is no proof of such a collection with this or other preface or introduction. There is also the view that the purpose of Ephesians is to call the recipients back to baptism.[29] This view also is inadmissible, since baptism is rather peripheral in the structure of the epistle, relative to its content coverage.

Another proposition is that the primary purpose of the epistle is to explicate God's love to mankind. Heil's otherwise excellent text-centred, literary-rhetorical, and recipient-centred analysis of Ephesians utilizes love as the analytical framework. Presuming love to be the paramount theme of Ephesians, Heil contends that love should provide a framework for understanding the epistle. He proceeds to say that Paul's purpose is to empower the recipients to walk in love for the unity of all in Christ. Arguably, it is possible to see love as a major theme in the epistle; the love of God to the recipients, and the various exhortations for them to do all things in love. But it seems to me the theme of love is the context in which to execute the exhortations or to understand what God has done to the recipients, not really the primary purpose of the epistle.

There are other, rather more remote if not speculative proposals on the purpose of Ephesians, such as to provide encouragement to Christians who perceived themselves as oppressed by the demonic realm,[30] to address a spiritual crisis in the church,[31] or to vindicate Paul, after his death, as the apostle whom God appointed to preach the gospel to the Gentiles[32]—presuming here of course that the author of Ephesians was another person, not Paul.

A good number of interpreters suggest the purpose of the epistle to be in relation to life in the church. These include those who hold the view that the purpose was to combat alienating tendencies Gentile Christians must have been experiencing from Jewish Christians and the Jewish roots of Christianity;[33] or to reinforce the identity of the recipients as participants in the church, as well as underline their distinctive role and conduct in the world;[34] or that Paul intended to persuade the Ephesians to correct

28. For example Goodspeed, *Meaning of Ephesians*.
29. See for example Kirby, *Ephesians*, 145, 159.
30. See Arnold, *Ephesians*, 266.
31. See Schnackenburg, *Epistle*, 35.
32. See Kitchen, *Ephesians*, 129.
33. For example, Martin, Epistle in Search."
34. See Lincoln, *Ephesians*, xxxvi.

The Mature Church

their view of the church in favor of another, based on the *kyriarchal* family model;[35] or that the author seeks to exhort the recipients to uphold unity in the church.[36]

I argue that all these proposals are untenable. There is nothing in the epistle to suggest that Ephesians is a response to any special need on the part of the recipients, nor does it indicate that the recipients, on their side, had given Paul any particular occasion for writing it. From the text it is clear that Paul does not address himself anywhere to anyone else except the converted Gentiles. When Paul prays on their behalf (Eph 1:17ff.; 3:14ff.) he does not mention any particular danger from which he would have God deliver them. To suppose that Paul is addressing some tensions between Gentile Christians and Jewish Christians would not be admissible either, because even the section containing the exhortations to unity (Eph 2:2ff.) does not suggest or imply the existence of any antagonism among those to whom he is writing, and there is no question of the reproduction or re-establishment of unity.

Thus, the purpose of Ephesians needs to be established, and this is to be done by examining the structure of the epistle and the flow of the argument. Paul's focus first is to provide the Ephesians with full knowledge of the blessings that, through God's great love and grace, they have acquired in Christ, despite their pagan origin. All the exhortations given pertain to the pagan origin as well as the new nature of the recipients. Clearly, there is an invitation extended to the recipients to understand and appreciate, as well as celebrate God's plan for their redemption and all its benefits. In addition, the purpose is to induce the Gentile Christians to reject the Jew-Gentile distinction, because they are now united and are together destined to be brought into full conformity with the image of Christ, and to live lives that are commensurate with their identity as exalted into the dignity status of sons of God.

In his analysis, Jeal suggests that the comparison of the "then" and "now" of the Gentile Christians implies a progression. The recipients are a "building" that is growing, or meant to be growing, to become the "temple of God."[37] Jeal argues that there is also progression in Paul's word use: at first the recipients have moved from "those besides a house" to become "those who belong to a house" or "members of the family" (2:19), and thereafter

---

35. Kittredge, *Community and Authority*, 146

36. For example Lloyd-Jones, *Christian Unity*; Stott, *Message*; O'Brien, *Epistle*; Lincoln, *Ephesians*.

37. Jeal, "Rhetorical Argumentation," 314.

not as members of the house, but they become the house itself, "built on a foundation" (Eph 2:20). They are now "a building" (2:21), and they are "being built" (2:22) to "become a dwelling place" (2:22) of God.[38] This progression signifies Paul's desire for the spiritual maturity of the recipients.

The purpose of inviting the recipients to grow towards maturity is also reflected in 3:14-19. Paul's prayer is for the Father to strengthen the believers in the "inner person" so that Christ dwells in their hearts, they understand the dimensions of the love of Christ, and they be filled with the fullness of God. Paul explains that Christ gave gifts to the believers (4:7-12) and behavior that would promote unity among believers, with the ultimate goal that the believers reach the unity of the faith and in the knowledge of the Son of God, become mature, attaining the whole measure of the fullness of Christ (4:13). With such maturity, the recipients would no longer be infants, a condition that constitutes—leads or contributes to—instability (see 4:14); instead, each member would function effectively to the benefit of the overall continuing maturity of the body. Furthermore, with such maturity the believers would be able to recognize and withstand and refuse or confront false teachings. They would, instead, be able to lead lives according to the standards set and be ready for spiritual warfare (6:10-17). Again, there are progressive changes in the imagery, from "building" to "body" to "battle," but the notion of strength and maturity is still the same. The exhortations in 4:17—6:9 in deference of relationships, including speech, work, anger, resisting the devil, and relationships at the work place and in the family, are standards of behavior, but also all could be seen as aspects of growth and maturity expected or required of the recipients.

From this analysis of the epistle, it becomes clear that there is a rhetorical purpose. That purpose is to urge and instruct the recipients to know and celebrate their identity, to grow towards maturity, and to live according to their identity. The author's concern is for the recipients' growth, maturation, and Christian behavior and encourages the recipients through a rhetorical argument that is designed to shape their thinking that way. Analysis of the structure of epistle will bring to the fore the relationship between the identity of the recipients, their spiritual growth and maturity, and the express behavior required of them.

---

38. Ibid., 321.

3.3 Rhetorical Structure of Ephesians

To do a rhetorical-critical analysis of a biblical text, or of any other text, presumes the particular text is an argument. To this effect, important questions are to be asked with regard to Ephesians. Is Ephesians an argument? How does the author present the argument? What is the rhetorical situation? What rhetorical strategy does the author employ? What end results does Paul seek to achieve in the recipients?[39] By addressing such questions, the rhetorical structure of the epistle is examined and identified.

Kern draws a conclusion of a survey of supposed progenitors of Paul among the early Christian writers on the language of Paul's letters, stating that "claims of a rhetorical approach to Paul contained in certain recent works may require rethinking. As classical and patristic scholars have observed, the earliest Christians found in Paul no rhetorician or high-born orator but a humble author of weighty letters."[40] However, that is not to say Paul's letters should not be analyzed using rhetorical-critical and rhetorical-analytical methods. Paul would have been familiar with the three primary types of speeches in classical rhetorical theory, namely epideictic, deliberative, and judicial rhetoric.[41] He would also be familiar with the epistolary conventions. With the flourishing rhetorical tradition of the first century AD, it is unlikely a person of Paul's education and social standing would have escaped the influence of that tradition and there is no reason to believe that the influence did not come through in his writings. Indeed, Paul employs all of these types, to different degrees, in the epistle, as he does in other epistles, particularly Romans, 1 Corinthians, and Galatians.[42] Even if it were granted that Paul may not have written his letter like a rhetorician, since his letters are with us it is possible to analyze them on their own merits utilizing rhetorical-critical and rhetorical-analytical approaches.

---

39. These or similar questions are also raised by others who have analyzed the rhetorical argumentation of Ephesians, e.g. Jeal, "Rhetorical Argumentation," 311.

40. Kern, *Rhetoric and Galatians*, 203.

41. Epideictic rhetoric pertains to giving speeches of "appraisal" as commendation, praise, and appreciation or blame, both in their own sake but also to invite the audience to appropriate participation in the same. Deliberative rhetoric pertains to the presentation of arguments—employing in any appropriate combination of logos, ethos, and pathos—to invite or influence the audience to consider and respond in line with the desire of the speaker or author. Judicial rhetoric pertains to the use of arguments within the framework of establishing justice, usually in a court of law or legal proceeding.

42. See Stowers, *Reading of Romans*; Sullivan & Anibile, "Epideictic Dimension."

Obviously, it would not be proper or safe to impose a rhetorical-critical scheme into which a letter does not fit. For example, if the letter does not have a clear structure, to analyze it using the Greco-Roman rhetorical species—*exordium, narration, proposition, probation, exortatio and peroration*—would be an improper imposition. But there is no threat in looking at a text from the new rhetorical criticism perspective, where a rhetorical-critical analysis is done to identify the rhetorical dimensions of the text, such as author, authorial intent or purpose, recipient, desired recipient response, and the rhetorical situation.

As noted earlier, in general, Ephesians is widely considered as having two main sections, namely, chapters 1–3 and chapters 4–6. However, a careful reading of the epistle shows that it has three distinct sections and therefore leads to a rejection of the bifocal view of the epistle. In following the bifocal view of the structure of the epistle, some scholars have failed to see the interdependent connection of chapters 1–3 and 4–6, and others have even denied any such connection. More obviously, the key aspects in 4:1–16 do not seem to belong at the same level as the other aspects of Ephesians 4–6. Clearly, 1:1—3:21 is distinct, presenting the doctrinal aspects and inviting the recipients to know and celebrate their new identity. Section 4:1–16 is also clearly distinct, presenting a specific theme and constituting a link between the first section and the third section. The third section of the letter, which is also clearly distinct, is 4:17—6:21, presenting standards of behavior on a number of levels and pertaining to a variety of spheres of life. My proposition is that the structure of Ephesians consists of three, not two, major sections: chapters 1–3; 4:1–16; and 4:17–6:21.

In view of the discussion above, the outline of the Epistle is as follows:

3.3.1 Outline of Ephesians

Saved to Fulfill Christian Responsibility from Maturity

1 **GREETINGS (1:1, 2)**

2 **KNOW AND CELEBRATE YOUR NEW IDENTITY (1:3—3:21)**
    2.1   Saints, faithful, in Christ (1:1b)
    2.2   God defined the identity before the foundation of the world (1:3–16)

The Mature Church

- 2.3 The transaction is complete and final (1:17–23)
- 2.4 "Then" and "now" (2:1–22)
  - 2.4.1 You were dead, now you are alive (2:1–10)
  - 2.4.2 You were excluded, now you are included in and through Christ (2:11, 12)
  - 2.4.3 You were far, now you are nearer (2:14)
  - 2.4.4 There was hostility, now there is peace (2:15–18)
  - 2.4.5 No longer foreigners and aliens, now you are in God's house with his people (2:19–22)
- 2.5 God included you in his eternal plan (3:1–13)
  - 2.5.1 God appointed me for you (3:1–6)
  - 2.5.2 Mystery was hidden, now God's wisdom is manifest through the church (3:7–13)
- 2.6 Know this God and be filled with his fullness (3:14–21)
- 2.7 An exaltation of this God (3:20–21)

3 GROW TO MATURITY (4:1–16)

- 3.1 Remember your new identity, and live accordingly (4:1–6)
- 3.2 Grow to maturity (4:7–15)
  - 3.2.1 Christ has provided the resources for you to grow into maturity (4:7–12)
  - 3.2.2 The ultimate goal of maturity (4:13)
  - 3.2.3 The imperative and indicators of maturity (4:14–15)

4 FULFIL YOUR RESPONSIBILITY AS CHRISTIANS (4:17—6:20)

- 4.1 Therefore, from now on (4:17)
- 4.2 Radically new standards of personal behavior (4:18—5:20)
- 4.3 Radically new standards of personal relationships (5:21—6:9)
  - 4.3.1 Mutual submission (5:21)
  - 4.3.2 Husbands and wives (5:22–33)
  - 4.3.3 Children and parents (6:1–4)
  - 4.3.4 Slaves and masters (6:5–9)
- 4.4 Capability and preparedness for the spiritual conflict (6:10–20)

5 CONCLUSION, FINAL GREETINGS, AND BENEDICTION (6:21-24)

3.3.2 The New Identity of the Gentile Christians (Eph 1-3)[43]

The recipients have a new identity, which they are to know and understand and which, consequently, they are to celebrate. They are to know its source, its multiple dimensions, and its essence.

3.3.2.1 Blessed be God: Invitation to celebrating God's wonder

There are excellent analyses of this doctrinal section of the epistle.[44] In general, these analyses show that the body of believers was formed in eternity past, for God's purpose and this should send humankind celebrating. Ephesians opens with a jubilant summary of Pauline thought (1:3-14). The Apostle sets forth the supreme worth of Christianity, suggesting that the Christian experience is nothing less than a new life through the grace of God (2:1-10). The death of Christ has opened to the Gentiles a way to God (2:11-22) and they now have full rights in Christianity (3:1-13). In a prayerful appeal the Apostle sets forth the greatness of the Christian's experience of Christ's love, and an exultant doxology marks the conclusion of the first main part of the epistle (3:14-21).

As Briscoe (1978) notes, the Apostle Paul barely gets through the introduction of the epistle to the church in Ephesus before he gets into profound expression of appreciation to God—in my view, a typical epideictic rhetoric: "Blessed be the God the Father of our Lord Jesus Christ" (1:3). As Briscoe (1978:7) explains, "blessed be," εὐλογητός, shows how the Gentile Christians, like all others of course, are to think highly and then speak highly of God. Paul's utter excitement is probably a product of a profound

---

43. From a rhetorical criticism perspective, the rhetorical genre of this section is epideictic or demonstrative rhetoric. By its character and function, epideictic rhetoric is meant to praise (or blame, as may be appropriate) or to appraise and invite the audience to join in doing the same (cf. Kern, *Rhetoric and Galatians*; 35). Paul seeks to persuade the audience to adopt or reaffirm some point of view in the present, so to praise or blame a person or quality (see O'Brien, *Epistle*, 74; Aristotle, *Rhetoric*, 46ff.). A strategy he is using in the epideictic rhetoric is to enlarge the contrast between the then and the now of the audience, using the language of extremes; for example, you were once dead but you are now alive.

44. See Scott, *Methods*; MacArthur, *Ephesians*; Boice, *Ephesians*; Hodge, *Ephesians*, 25-120; O'Brien, *Epistle*.

understanding of God himself with particular reference to his dealings with mankind through Christ. The major point Paul is making here is that this new identity they now have, God worked out for them before the foundations of the world and, amazingly, without their knowledge.

There is a broad usage of the term "to bless" here. In effect, Paul says that God thinks so highly of mankind that he commanded that certain things be done for them—thus blessing them. It is an utter declaration of the absolute goodness of God. God is both the blessed one and the one who blesses.[45] Paul explains to the recipients what God did for them long before their existence, and therefore without their knowledge, so that they now have this new identity. God has acted according to the good pleasure of his will (1:5) and now God has made known to them the mystery of his will (1:9).

Paul writes that the blessing of God was part of the plan of God and this plan predated human existence and the foundation of the world (1:4). God showed the Gentile Christians his grace, as "riches" and "glory." The recipients would understand that grace is far greater than justice and mercy. Whereas justice administers what a person deserves, and mercy delivers a person from all that the person deserves, grace bestows upon a person what the person will never deserve. Justice is where a stern judge is sitting on his bench, administering the law. Mercy is the situation whereby that same judge—feeling the pain of the guilty one, understanding his problems, recognizing extenuating circumstances—gives the lightest possible punishment. But grace is the judge removing his robes of office, standing with the offender, paying the fine, and leading the guilty party out of court to the judge's own home and to be a member of the family, with all the rights and privileges of family membership. Paul calls these rights and privileges "all spiritual blessings in Christ" (1:3). This suggests that mercy without grace is both inadequate to meet human need and a rather inadequate expression of God's character. God showed the Gentile Christians his grace, not mercy.

3.3.2.2 New identity of the Gentile Christians

Paul presents an inherent invitation to the recipients to understand and join him in celebrating their new identity. They are now saints, faithful and in Christ, and it is all by the wonderful doing of God (1:1–2). In this new identity, which was formed from eternity past through divine election

---

45. Cf. MacArthur, *Ephesians*, 7.

(1:4–6a), the Gentile Christians around Ephesus were also included when they heard the Gospel of salvation (1:13) and, having believed, they were marked in Christ with a seal, the Holy Spirit (1:13). The Spirit is the pledge[46] of our inheritance (1:14). Not only were the recipients previously unable to participate in attaining this identity, but they in fact were ignorant of what was going on long before they existed. He presents the deeds of God, for the recipients, so the recipients would join in the praise of God.

Paul articulates the spiritual blessings of God to the human race, locatable only in the heavenly places (1:3). In the same way that the atmosphere is full of electromagnetic waves of which we are totally unaware until we tune in television or radio sets, so is the natural world permeated with the unseen, unknown world of the heavenly places. Many people know nothing of this world of spiritual delight and blessing and they never will unless they are tuned into the wavelength of the heavenly places. The tuning process takes place solely by means of being in Christ. Christ is much like a computer flash drive into which God has saved all the blessings, awaiting anyone to download them by being in Christ. Thus, besides the presentation of Christ to the recipients instrumentally,[47] Christ too is presented in a manner as to invite the recipients to join in the praise of him.

As part of that identity in Christ, God has adopted the recipients to sonship and they now have full status as sons, including being heirs of God through Christ (cf. Rom 8:15; Gal 4:7). In Christ God has chosen them that they would live before him holy and without blemish. In Christ, the human race, including the Gentile Christians, has "redemption[48] through

46. Ἀρραβών is a Semitic word signifying a downpayment. In the Hellenistic Greek it became the ordinary commercial term for first installment, guaranteeing future ownership. In the New Testament writings it is used only in the epistles of Paul and always in reference to the Holy Spirit (see O'Brien, *Epistle*, 120–21). Best (1998, *Critical and Exegetical*, 151) explains that in this particular case the Holy Spirit is regarded not so much as the tool that causes the mark on the object being sealed, but as the very mark that is left on the object. The sealing indicates that the recipients belong to God and are under his protection.

47. Best (*Critical and Exegetical*, 154) explains that for Paul the phrase "in Christ" has two thrusts, the instrumental and the local. In the instrumental usage, God is now introduced more explicitly as the subject of action in Christ benefiting believers.

48. MacArthur (*Ephesians*, 17, 18) explains that the word "redemption" comes from one of six terms taken from the field of law and used in the New Testament in relation to salvation. Διακιόω and related terms refer to legal acquittal of a charge; theologically used to refer to the repentant sinner's forgiveness and subsequent vindication, justification, and declaration of righteousness before God, as in Rom 3:4; 4:25; 5:18; and 1 Tim 3:16. Ἀφίημι basically is used in reference to legal debt cancellation and repayment or the

The Mature Church

his blood" (1:7). Ἀπολύτρωσις (redemption), from λυτρόω, in Paul's day literally meant "to loose from" and was used to describe freeing of prisoners of war, slaves, and criminals condemned to death. The idea is the ransom being paid to deliver those incapable of freeing themselves. The human race was naturally incapable of freeing itself from the bondage of sin and its consequences, but in Christ God delivered us. Furthermore, as a result of redemption, in Christ God has forgiven the human race, including Gentile Christians. It is the ἄφεσις—the remission of sins—not forgiveness (1:7b—9a). As the compassionate creditor forgave the poor debtor (Matt 18:27), God has moved with compassion towards the unworthy Gentiles and has removed from them the obligation to pay for their trespasses, and his forgiveness is infinite.[49] In Christ God has enriched them, and so Gentile Christians, like the rest of the believing human race, are now honored to have become the special possession of God. And finally, in Christ, God will gather the Gentile Christians. In the fullness of time (1:10) God will bring everything to a climax, when he will gather all things to himself, and the divine inheritance is guaranteed (1:11–14), sealed in the Holy Spirit, who is given as a pledge of that inheritance (1:14a).

So the Gentile Christians too have a new identity and a new status. Paul also, through his petition for them, implies what else could become of them: receiving from God the spirit of wisdom and revelation in the knowledge of him (1:17); having the eyes of their hearts enlightened to know the hope of God's calling and the riches of the glory of his inheritance in the saints (1:18); understanding of the greatness of God's power (1:19–20); and understanding the greatness of God's person (1:21–23).

---

granting of a pardon over a debt; theologically it is used to refer to God's forgiveness of sin (cf. Matt 9:2; Rom 4:7; Eph 1:7; 4:32). Υἱοθεσία refers to the legal process of adopting a child and is used by the Apostle Paul to represent the believer's adoption into the family of God (see Rom 8:15; Gal 4:5; Eph 1:5). Καταλλάσσω means to legally reconcile two parties in dispute at a court of law, used in the New Testament to refer to the believer's reconciliation with God through Jesus Christ (cf. Rom 5:10; 2 Cor 5:18–20). Ἀγοράζω and ἐξαγοράζω, two related Greek legal terms, refer to buying or purchasing. The source, ἀγορά, means marketplace. In the New Testament, the related words are used to refer to spiritual purchase or redemption (cf. Gal 3:13; Rev 5:9; 14:3–4). Λυτρόω is the other Greek word for redemption, and along with its related terms means to release from captivity. It carried an even stronger connotation than ἀγοράζω. It is the word rendered in the English translation as "redemption," the word used to refer to the paying of a ransom in order to release a person from bondage, especially slavery.

49. MacArthur, *Ephesians*, 25.

3.3.2.3 *"Then" but "now"*

A second major doctrinal category of the Apostle's engagement is the new state of the recipients. He especially underlines this new identity by absolute contrast of the past and present conditions of the recipients. They were once all dead but now they are alive (2:1–10). The emphasis is the fact of sinfulness and salvation from sin (2:1–3); that is to say, they were sinners not because they were sinning but rather they were sinning because they were sinners. In their former condition, they were in sin, controlled by the supernatural evil powers, and were actually governed by wrong desires, and by that fact they were spiritually dead. The emphasis is that apart from Christ man is in sin, and because man is in sin man is dead. Both the παράπτωματα (trespasses) and the ἁρμάτιαι (sins) are consequences and manifestations of the sinful human condition, before they personally came to Christ in faith.

Paul goes on to teach that salvation is on the basis of God's love (2:4), that salvation means moving from death into life (2:5), and that salvation is with a purpose (2:6, 7). Paul further teaches in this epistle that salvation is by faith and only by faith (2:8), not by works; and that salvation is for good works (2:10). The implication here is that for salvation good works have absolutely no value, but after salvation good works are absolutely necessary. Thus, the state of the Ephesians before their conversion is spiritual death, which in turn includes a state of sin, a state of subjection to Satan and human corruption, and a state of condemnation (2:1–3).[50] But as a result of believing in Christ, the recipients have undergone a radical change, and that change is spiritual resurrection (2:4–6).

Paul teaches that *formerly* these recipients were excluded, but now they are included in and through Christ (2:11, 12). As Gentiles by birth or by lack of physical circumcision, they were separated from Christ, excluded from citizenship in Israel,[51] and foreigners to the covenant of the promise. *Formerly* they were without hope and without God in the world (2:12), a

---

50. The idea is not that people are born alive and slowly die through sinning and are then made alive again at conversion, or that they begin by being spiritually alive and then die because of sin; it is not a process of slow dying or moral degeneration as such. This is Paul's theological judgment on the preconversion of all. People are born dead and remain so until they come to believe in Christ (Best, *Critical and Exegetical*, 201).

51. They now share Israel's privilege, which they previously did not. As they have entered the heritage of Israel (O'Brien, *Epistle*, 183), they can now share God's covenant with Israel in Genesis 12:1–3 and they can now understand the language of divine promises and covenantal provisions.

state that meant they were far away (2:13a). *But now*, through Christ, they have been brought near (2:13b). The previous dispensation also meant hostility and separation, being away from God and outside the household of God, and incompatible with the temple of God (cf. 2:14). *But now*, with this dispensation, there is a change in the relationship between the Gentiles and God, between the Gentiles and the Jews, and between them all and God. The Gentile Christians *are now* part of the body, as a result of the peace-making work of Christ (2:14-18). *Now*, after believing Christ, they have been brought near through his blood; *now* they are no longer foreigners and aliens but fellow citizens with God's people (2:19). *Now* the Gentiles are heirs with Israel, members of one body and sharing in the promise of Christ (3:6). *Now* they are members of God's household (2:19, 20). There is no longer disunity, no (or ought not to be) social or spiritual alienation among all the Ephesians; there is unity in Christ (2:13-18) and they are at peace with God and with God's people (2:14-17). Christ has made them a new people—new καινός, meaning, they are now different in kind and quality. Not that they have simply been proselytized into the commonwealth of Israel, but rather a transformation has taken place and they have become members of a newly created community that transcends Israel, with its privileges, and they are on equal footing with the Jews who believe (see O'Brien 1999:191). The Gentile believers are now united in God's kingdom (2:19b), united in God's household (2:19b), and united in God's temple (2:20-22).

3.3.2.4 *God included you in his eternal plan (3:1-13)*

The new identity is in fact part of God's grand plan. So 3:1-13 is an explication of Paul's ministry foreordained specifically to be an apostle to the Gentiles (3:1-6) and that the entire mystery was to be revealed everywhere through a divinely determined mechanism called the church. As the Apostle Paul speaks of his apostleship in this section, the reason is not to defend it against any attacks but to express all his gratitude to this loving God for having called him, in spite of his unworthiness, to announce the great mystery—and to the Gentiles for that matter. Paul seeks to underscore his special role in the move of the Gentile Christians from paganism to Christianity (2:1-10) and also into the people of God (2:11-22). It is like he is saying that God would do everything, and nothing would stand in his way to have his plan for the Gentiles fulfilled.

From a rhetorical strategy point of view, intended or unintended, this may be proof of ethos, that is, Paul is establishing his ethos, as a means to invite the recipients to consider his claims in the preceding sections appropriately. Paul's ministry to them as Gentiles is God-given, and he accepts and he appreciates it as such. That being the case, Paul is both a legitimate and an authoritative figure to explain to them their new identity and, later, give exhortations because of that new identity. It is possible, as Jeal suggests,[52] that in explaining the "mystery" Paul would be applying pathos, to persuade the recipients to see their collective security as Christians and engender an understanding on their part that they are joint participants in the gospel (3:6). However, Jeal's suggestion that Paul's goal in stating his concerns about the recipients is to persuade the recipients to accept his authority to speak and, subsequently, get stimulated to accept his yet-to-come exhortations on maturity and growth, would not be admissible. There is no reason to believe Paul needed to cultivate acceptance of his authority as such to the recipients. Rather, he is simply reinforcing the recipients' understanding of what he has been saying to and about them up to that point, namely, that they have a new identity and a new state; but now he adds that all this is part of a divine mystery in which God included them as well. That means that the preparedness of the recipients to receive favorably what Paul is going to say next—exhorting them to maturity (in 4:1–16) and to live by new standards (in 4:17—6:20)—was not going (and did not have) to be based on Paul's authority but on their new identity and their new state, as Gentile Christians. The mystery was hidden, but now God's wisdom is manifest through the church (3:7–13). Secondarily, this also provides information on the nature or essence and responsibility of the church universal.

3.3.2.5 Know this God and be filled with his fullness (3:14–21)

In this section Paul says that he prays for the recipients to desire and to be filled with the fullness of God. This God is not only the God of a grand plan but is in fact great and powerful and able to provide beyond human comprehension. The impact of such a prayer and the doxology (3:20, 22) on the recipients would include a confidence in God and a willingness to identify with and worship God.

---

52. Jeal, "Rhetorical Argumentation," 323.

They have a new identity and a new status. They have moved from a degrading heathen condition to a state of dignity bestowed upon them by God through Christ. They are on a firm foundation for new existence, established by God from eternity past by his love and extended to them and all humanity by his grace. The Gentile Christians are now invited to marvel at what God has made them to be and to celebrate their new status based on their new identity.

3.3.3   The Necessary Middle (4:1–16)

This is the second major section of the epistle. In this section Paul exhorts the recipients to live their lives in a manner worthy of their calling. Since he begins the section with "therefore," he must be linking what he is going to write next to what he has written so far. The first verse of the section, 4:1, implies at least two important things. First, the new identity that the recipients have is to be understood as a divine calling they have received. As a matter of principle, they are to be completely humble and gentle, patient and bearing one another in love (4:2), and they are to make every effort to keep the unity of the Spirit through peace (4:3). Paul restates their new identity already communicated to them earlier: there is still one body and one Spirit; one Lord, one faith, and one baptism (4:4); and one God and Father of all (4:6). Secondly, this divine calling, or this new identity, has perpetual implications for living. It means that who they now are places responsibility upon them.

Paul then explains that each individual among the recipients has unique gifts, received from Christ, to contribute so that they all can pattern their lives in accordance with their calling. There are different functional offices and different levels of organizing the functions. To start with, Christ, the Head, has appointed and anointed human beings to various positions, and their collective and overall task is to equip or prepare the saints so that the body is built. In turn, the individual saints, who are another level of functioning, would contribute accordingly to the further building of the body (4:11–12).

When everything has happened as it should, there will be maturity. Hence, the goal of Christ's provision of gifting resources and ministry appointments is to bring about maturity (4:13). The full maturity has its dimensions: unity in the faith in the Son of God, personal knowledge of the Son of God, and attaining to the whole measure of the fullness of Christ.

There are indicators of such maturity: stability against false doctrines, capability to resist being tossed by the waves and being blown by every wind of false teaching, capability to recognize and resist craftiness and cunning of men and the scheming of Satan, orientation and ability to speak the truth in love (4:16), and the proper functioning of every member (4:16). With maturity, they will now no longer be infants. It is only then that they can pursue the responsibility of their new identity, as described in 4:17—6:20.

3.3.4 Responsibility in the New Identity (4:17—6:20)

In this third and last main section of the epistle, Paul exhorts the recipients to conduct themselves according to their new identity, to fulfill their *Christian responsibility*. In general, there are new standards for personal conduct (4:17—5:20); there are new and radically different standards for relationships in all of life (5:22—6:9), governed by a new principle (5:21); and finally, they are in battle and they had better be in full armor for perpetual combat against spiritual forces (6:10-20).

Broadly speaking, four aspects constitute Christian responsibility, according to this passage. The first is holy living (4:17-19). The world in which the recipients live is a system or a pattern not designed or fitting for them. The pagans follow the futility of their thinking, they are darkened in their understanding, and they are separated from God because of the πώρωσις (hardening) of their hearts (4:17-18). It is this condition of the pagan world that governs the conduct of the pagans. The Gentile Christians are exhorted to "no longer live as the pagans do" (4:17); instead, they are to live as they have come to know Christ (4:20). This is an emphasis that the new life they are to live can only come forth from the knowledge of Christ and his ways in the deepest, most personal, and most profound sense.

The second aspect is to "put off" the old conduct and "put on" the new conduct (4:22-32), that is, to abandon the former pagan ways and adopt Christian standards of behavior. After taking off the "former way of life" and "the old self, which is being corrupted by its deceitful desires" (4:23), they are to assume a life patterned after the standards he gives. They are to put off lying and put on speaking truthfully (4:25); put off anger—referring to uncontrolled, selfish or sinful anger; put off stealing and work hard to fend for themselves and others (4:28); put off unwholesome talk so that instead every word they speak is beneficial to those who hear it (4:29); and put off bitterness, rage, and malice, and instead show love (4:31, 32). These

The Mature Church

aspects of conduct are to be the standards of a people with a new identity, and they are to be the standards because they reflect the character of Christ (5:1-2). The recipients are exhorted not to allow even suspicion of sexual immorality among them; that means none of them should be sexually immoral (5:3). They must give up their old sins and live in the new light (5:3-21).

The third aspect is the new standards for organizing relationships. Under the new general principle of mutual submission (5:21), the marriage relation among them must truly symbolize the union of Christ with the church (5:22-33). Children, parents, slaves, and masters have their special duties as Christians (6:1-9). And finally (6:10), they all are to put on the Christian armor and perpetually remain on duty in spiritual warfare (6:10-20)—a serious call to duty from which no one is exempt.

There are those scholars who hold the view that Ephesians does not have any argument,[53] but I contend that they are missing it. As the analysis of the argument of Ephesians has revealed, Paul seeks to influence the recipients in a particular way. From the analysis of the argument of Ephesians, it is evident that Paul has an agenda for the recipients to consider and respond in line with his view. To that effect, Ephesians presents a primary argument, evidencing an authorial intention for the recipients. That argument is that the Gentile Christians, by the grace of God through the saving death of Christ, have a new identity. They should celebrate that identity and perpetually praise God for it. They have a responsibility to live according to new standards, radically different from their former ways and the ways of the contemporary pagans. This behavior is to be an expression of the new identity and state of the Gentile Christians. This behavior is both a response to what God has done in Christ and a proper accompaniment to the praise of God in view of what he has done for the Gentile Christians.[54] This is the *Christian responsibility* in society and in the world in general.

However, in order to be able to live in accordance with the new set of standards of behavior, the Ephesians must grow to full spiritual maturity. Spiritually immature members not only will deny the rest of the family their contribution of meaningful service, but they might even be detrimental to the very existence and progress of the rest of the Christian family.

---

53. Among them are Best, *Critical and Exegetical*; Lincoln, *Ephesians*; O'Brien, *Epistle*; and Muddiman, *Commentary*.

54. See Best, *Critical and Exegetical*, 353.

Communicative Function of Ephesians 4:1–16

The argument is therefore simply this: because the Ephesians have a new identity, they must grow to full spiritual maturity and live according to the new standards commensurate with that new identity. Therefore, Jeal's observation[55] that to speak of "an argument in Ephesians is immediately problematic," and the broad variation in scholarly interpretation "regarding what Ephesians is about, how it functions, and whether it is an argument at all," may well lie in the variation in conceptualization of argument and what constitutes argument or how argumentation is achieved.[56]

3.4 The Place of 4:1–16 in Ephesians

As I have proposed and elaborated, the epistle has three primary sections. The first, 1:1—3:21, spells out the new identity and new state of the Gentile Christians in greater Ephesus, to whom the Apostle Paul is writing. By the love and grace of God, they who were once dead, outside the covenantal promises, far from Christ, and without God in the world are now alive, forgiven, reconciled to Christ and to other believers, and have become part of the family of God, part of the building and the dwelling temple of God. They are now out of the fateful degradation of their former hopeless heathen condition of being lost in sin. As such they have acquired, by the bestowal of God, a new nature, a new status and, hence, a new identity. They are recipients of all the spiritual blessings of God and they are the blessed people of God, just like the Jewish Christians or any of those who became Christians first. Paul refers to this new identity as a calling (4:1).

The third section, 4:17—6:20, spells out the new standards of personal as well as communal behavior and relationships in the household: in marriage, between parents and children, and at the work place, specifically between the slave owners and slaves. This is a radical change in behavior that is to be completely different and strange to the system and pattern of the pagans.

In between the two sections is the second section of 4:1–16. Thus, contrary to many an interpreter of the epistle who concludes that the purpose of 4:1–16 is unity, my proposition is that the primary purpose of this section of the epistle is to call the recipients to *spiritual growth and full*

---

55. Jeal, "Rhetorical Argumentation," 310.
56. Incidentally, Jeal (ibid.) does not in this article define or explain his concept of "argument" or "argumentation," or that of other scholars to whom he is making reference on the subject.

The Mature Church

spiritual maturity. Being in the middle of the foundational articulation of the identity and state of the Christian, on the one hand, and his responsibility in everyday living, on the other hand, implies that spiritual maturity is central with regard to what a Christian is and does. Once one comes to the Christian faith one is called to participate in the Christian family in a manner that contributes to its overall growth.

Thus, 4:1–16 is the bridge between the two other primary sections of the epistle. Contrary to the view that the specific behavior of the paraenesis is not directly derived from the more theological description of chapters 1–3,[57] 4:1–16 provides the link between chapters 1–3 and 4:17—6:20. It seems clear from this section that *spiritual maturity* is the goal, that the spiritual gifting and establishment of ministerial offices are the means to spiritual maturity, and that without baptism there can be no maturity. I suggest that unity is a sign and expression of maturity (not the other way round) so that when all are mature there will be unity. However, there is a reference point, an ultimate standard of spiritual maturity, and that is: "till we all come in the unity of the faith, and of the knowledge of the Son of God, unto a perfect man, unto the measure of the stature of the fullness of Christ" (4:13). What is needed now is an interpretation of this verse, to which I turn in the next chapter.

3.5 Summary

In this chapter the rhetorical nature of Ephesians and the communicative function of 4:1–16 have been articulated, in order to set the stage for the interpretation of 4:13. It is clear from the analysis that the epistle has three primary sections, that is, 1:3—3:21, 4:1–16, and 4:17—6:20, dealing with Christian identity, spiritual maturity, and Christian responsibility, respectively. The three themes are sequentially dependent, such that spiritual maturity can only be realized within the context of Christian identity, and Christian responsibility is to be fulfilled through increasing spiritual maturity. Since the focus of the present study is 4:13, the next item of attention is to determine, in the next chapter, the meaning and various dimensions of spiritual maturity in 4:13.

---

57. See, for example, ibid., 324.

4

Meaning and Imperative of Christian Spiritual Maturity

4.1 Introduction

IN THIS CHAPTER, I argue that in Ephesians 4:1–16, the author underscores Christian spiritual maturity as the bridge between the new identity of the Christian (Eph 1–3) and the moral code of the Christian life commensurate with the new identity (4:17—6:20). I interpret Ephesians 4:13 to obtain the meaning of Christian spiritual maturity. Towards this end, I evaluate the most notable interpretations and views in relation to 4:13. Then, by way of a rhetorical-critical analysis of 4:13, I delineate the meaning of Christian spiritual maturity, and suggest its various implications. In the final analysis, I argue that, from its essence, Christian spiritual maturity is imperative and that it provides a basis for a renewed agenda on understanding and implementing effective discipleship Programs.

Ephesians 4:13 seems to be a New Testament basis for striving to reach Christian spiritual maturity. This is possibly the only passage in the New Testament where the ultimate goal of spiritual maturity is specified. A valid interpretation of this passage, to determine the meaning[1] of Christian spiritual maturity, as well as the implications of that meaning, is therefore called for.

1. "Meaning" can refer to what the author intended, what the recipient understood, or what meaning is encoded in the text. In a perfect communication situation, the author would have an intended meaning, correctly and adequately encoded and conveyed in the communicative devices the author is using, and since the communication process would have taken place in cognizance of the context of the recipient, the recipient would have decoded the meaning in a significantly correct way. Meaning would therefore have to be determined by analyzing the text from an understanding of both the author and the original recipient. This is the meaning of meaning in this article. For further discussion

The Mature Church

Although Ephesians was written in the first century AD, most likely AD 60 or 61, and in light of the realities of the first readers,[2] the epistle is as much relevant today as it was then. First, the basic truths are valid for people of all time: Since God's plan of redemption predates humanity, all peoples of all places and all time are covered by this everlasting stretch of the redemption plan and, therefore, also all those who will become believers. Thus the message of Ephesians is always alive and relevant.

As noted earlier on in this discussion, most researchers[3] on the epistle advance a two-section structure, 1:1—3:21 and 4:1—6:20, the one section presenting an articulation of the new identity of the gentiles and all its divine origins, and the other presenting the code of conduct for the new people. However, this manner of dividing the epistle reflects failure to notice that the code of conduct actually begins from 4:17. It is quite likely that it is this failure that led to treating 4:1–16 as a pericope on unity, in order to make it also an ethical matter. But analysis of the epistle reveals that the epistle has three primary sections. The first, 1:1—3:21, spells out the new identity and new state of the Gentile Christians to whom he is writing. The essence of the message is that by the love and grace of God, they who were once dead, outside the covenantal promises, far from Christ and without God in the world, are now alive, forgiven, reconciled to Christ and to other believers, have become part of the family of God, part of the building and the temple of God. They are now out of the fateful degradation of their former hopeless heathen condition of being lost in sin. As such they have acquired, by the bestowal of God, a new nature, a new status and, hence, a new identity, and they are an integral part of the church—the cosmic body of Christ. They are recipients of all the spiritual blessings of God and they are the blessed people of God like the Jewish Christians or any of those who became Christians first. Paul refers to this new identity as a calling (4:1).

---

on "meaning," see Klein, Blomberg, Hubbard, *Introduction to Biblical Interpretation* (2004), 8–13; cf. Marshall, "Introduction," 15.

2. Although the books of the New Testament were written with specific first readers in mind and, therefore, the human authors would have had specific purposes such as addressing specific issues that the first readers faced, the overall purposes of the books of the New Testament are applicable for all people of all time and place, to "hear what the Spirit is saying." Therefore, what is at issue is not the relevance of New Testament books but rather the task of interpreting and applying such texts.

3. Among them are Stott, *Message of Ephesians*; Lloyd-Jones, *Christian Unity*; Lincoln, *Ephesians*; Schnackenburg, *Epistle*; Best, *Critical and Exegetical*; O'Brien, *Epistle*; and Muddiman, *Commentary*.

Meaning and Imperative of Christian Spiritual Maturity

The third section, 4:17—6:20, spells out the standards of personal as well as communal behavior and relationships in the household for the Gentile Christians commensurate with their new identity: in marriage, between parents and children, at the work place specifically between the slave owners and slaves, their speech behavior and their work ethic. This is a radical change in behavior that is to be completely different and strange to the system and pattern of the Pagans. Paul is explicit in his call for the Gentile Christians to embrace this radical change from their hitherto way of life and invites them to do so with a sense of great celebration.

In between the two sections is the second section, 4:1–16. Thus, contrary to many an interpreter of the epistle who conclude that the purpose of 4:1–16 is unity, my proposition is that the primary purpose of this section is to call the recipients of this epistle to *spiritual growth and full spiritual maturity*. Being in the middle of the foundational articulation of the identity and state of the Christian, on the one hand, and Christian responsibility in everyday living, on the other, possibly implies that spiritual maturity is central with regard to what a Christian is and does.

The question, however, is: According to this pericope, what is the essence of Christian spiritual maturity and why is Christian spiritual maturity imperative, if it is? This is the problem that this chapter endeavors to address. To address the problem, I will first do a micro-level thought structure analysis of 4:1–16. I will thereafter evaluate the most salient interpretations of 4:13, after which I carry out a rhetorical-critical analysis of 4:13–16, to determine the meaning of spiritual maturity and, from that meaning, deduce its implications.

4.2 Thought Structure of 4:1–16

In order to be able to interpret 4:13, it is important that the syntactical function of the verse within the larger context of 4:1–16 is determined. Towards that end, a micro level analysis of the thought structure[4] of 4:1–16 is done.

---

4. The purpose of the analysis of thought structure on the micro level is to see how the syntactical units of the pericope of 4:1–16 are related to one another, in order to establish the syntactical function of 4:13. For explanation of the theory and procedure of thought structure and syntactical analysis, see Janse Van Rensburg, "Analysis of Syntactic Structure."

The Mature Church

4.2.1 The Thought Structure of 4:1–16 on a Micro Level

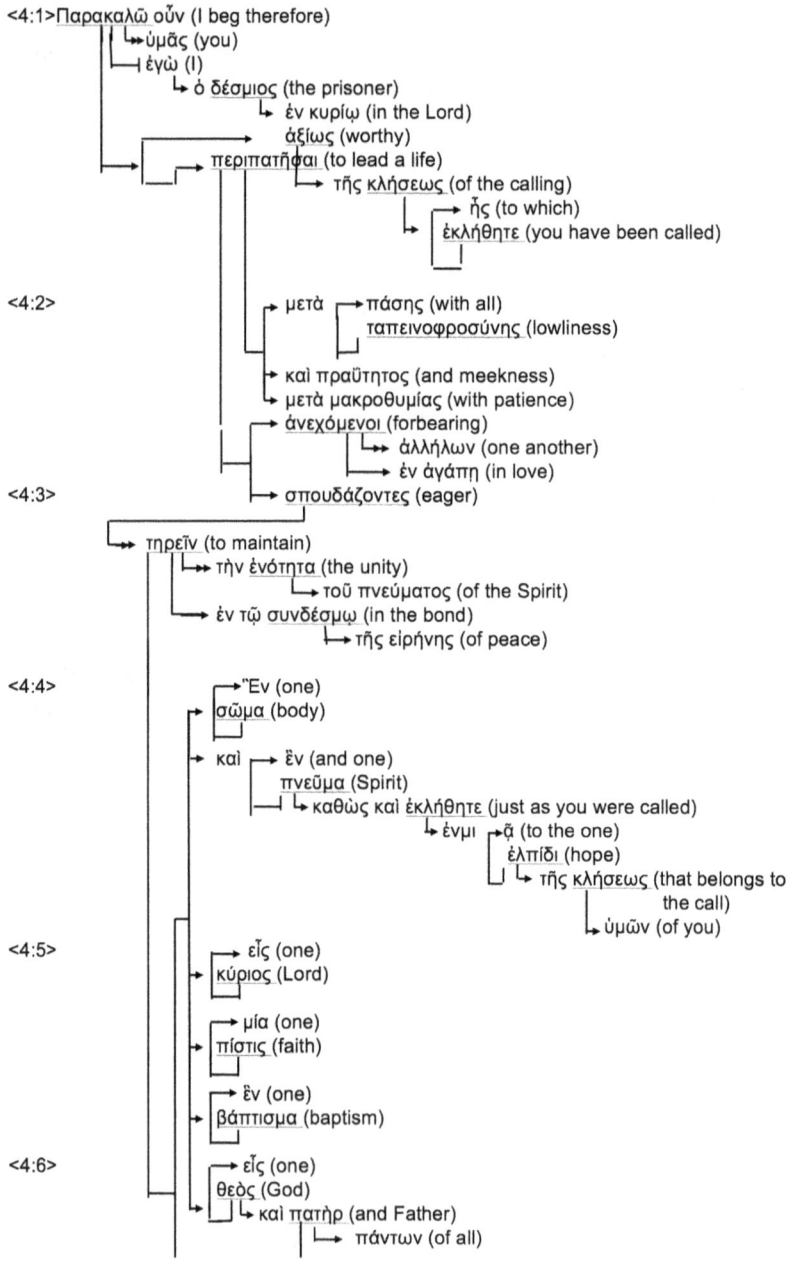

Meaning and Imperative of Christian Spiritual Maturity

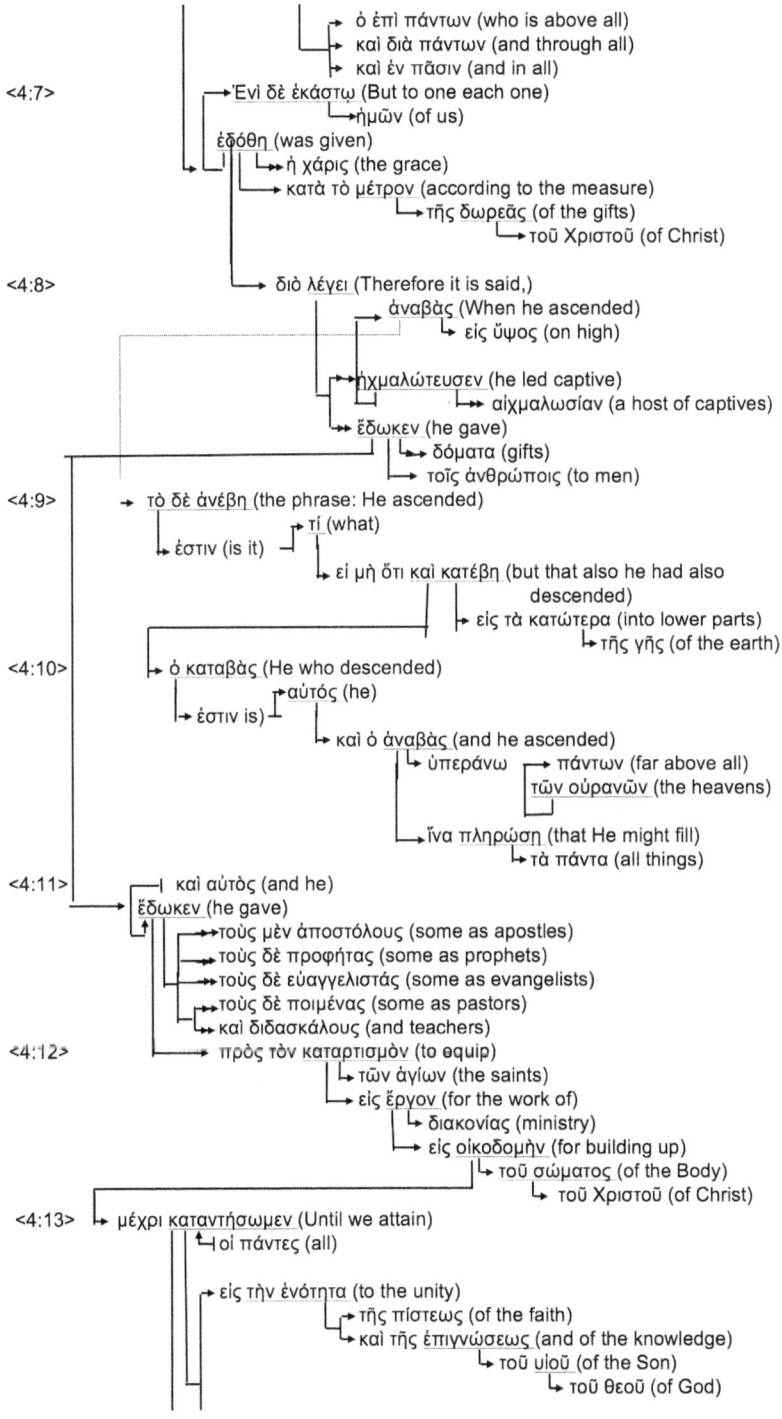

The Mature Church

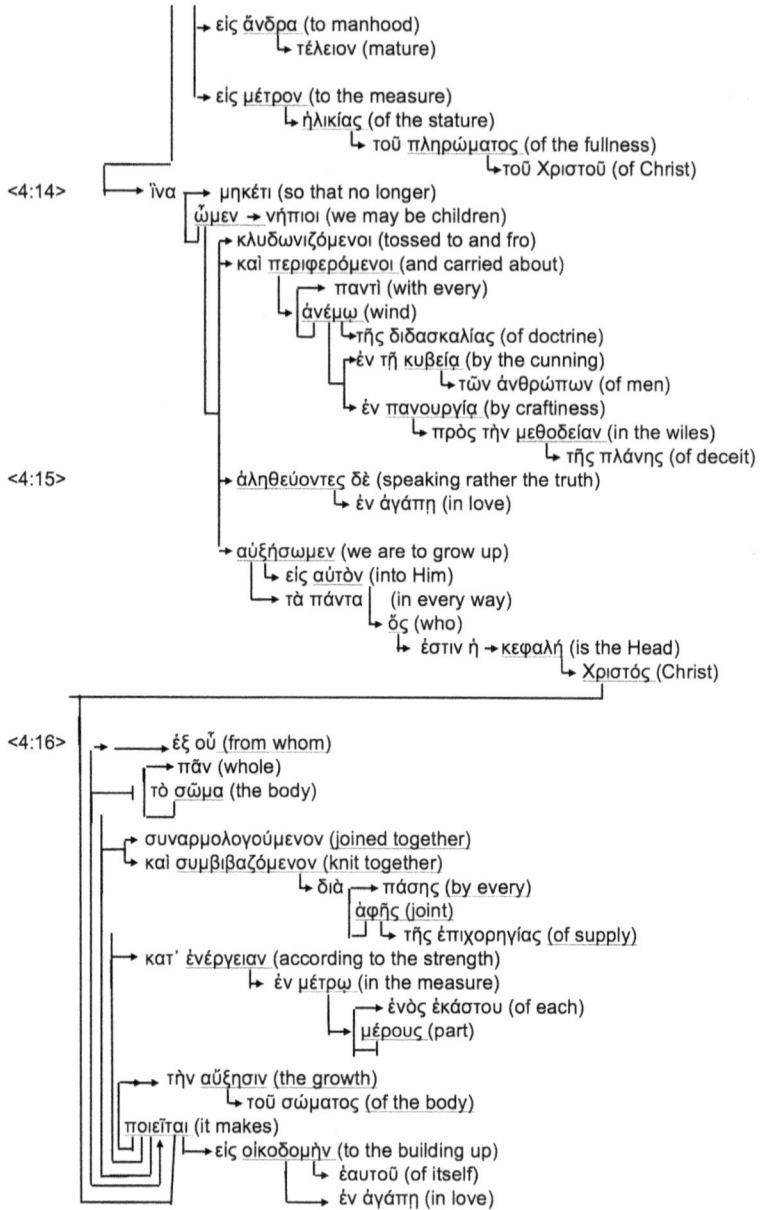

4.2.2 4:13 in the Context of 4:1–16

Since 4:13 is a long clause within a long sentence beginning from 4:11 and ending at 4:14, the interpretation of 4:13 requires taking into consideration this immediate textual context. But 4:11–14 is itself situated within 4:1–16, another broader immediate textual context necessary to consider in interpreting 4:13. Paul restates the fact that the recipients have received a calling, which is the new identity advanced in Ephesians 1–3; he urges them to therefore live accordingly (4:2) and reminds them of the oneness there is—one body, one Spirit, one hope, one Lord, one faith, one baptism, one God (4:4–6). Paul then introduces a new subject altogether, namely, what Christ has done and the purpose for which Christ has done it (4:7–10). He states that "to each one of us"—thus considering the recipients individually—grace has been given as Christ apportioned; he goes on to describe Christ, the giver of the grace.

Thereafter Paul states that Christ has given various gifts, which point to the various ministers he appointed and the objectives of these appointments (4:11). What follows in 4:12–14 are some clauses that have been a subject of wide discussion.[5] At issue in these discussions, first, is whether the clauses relate to the ministers or to Christ himself and, then, what relationship exists between the clauses. It is important to resolve these issues in order to determine the extent, if any, to which they inform a valid interpretation of 4:13. Three successive prepositional phrases follow after the statement that Christ appointed ministers (4:11) for the equipment of the saints, the work of the ministry, and building up the body of Christ. But how do these clauses relate to each other, and how do they pertain to the gifts Christ has given and the ministers he appointed?

From a review of the most pertinent literature on this question, three basic propositions can be constructed. However, as examination of each one of them will show, these propositions are not completely in harmony with the view that 4:1–16 is about Christian spiritual maturity. An alternative proposition is suggested, in section 4.2.6.

---

5. See, for example, Hendriksen, *Ephesians*, 197–201; Lincoln, *Ephesians*, 248–59; Schnackenburg, *Epistle*, 182–87.

4.2.3 The Parallel Proposition of the Three Clauses

In the parallel proposition, these clauses are seen as coordinates, all linked to "he gave," whereby the understanding is that Christ appointed the ministers in 4:11 to achieve all the three clauses, namely, "for the equipment of the saints," "for the work of the ministry," and "for building up of the body of Christ." Those who hold the view that the three clauses are parallel[6] argue that the clauses are non-dependent but are parallel and mutually reflect on each other, together building the total picture, with none of them more important than the others. The arguments in support of this view are that there are no grammatical or linguistic grounds to warrant or require making specific links between the three clauses. It is also argued that linking these clauses would constitute a clerically dominated interpretation, instead of emphasizing the active role and participation of all believers, and such dominating of the ministers would supposedly be contrary to 4:7 and 4:16.

However, this view does not persuade. The focus of 4:11 is clearly the ministers, not all believers, except believers as recipients of the ministry of the ministers. The fact that the active role of the believers is stated in 4:7 and 4:16 confirms that in 4:12 Paul's direct focus is on the ministers only. A desire for both a democratic view of church polity and a rejection of church hierarchy simply do not constitute a valid basis for the parallel view. I would argue further that on the basis of what is to follow the clauses, namely 4:13, a parallel proposition is not tenable. A parallel view of the three clauses would mean that the ministers are to continue working "for the equipment of the saints," "for the work of the ministry," and "for building up the body of Christ," until we all attain such full maturity that each member is meaningfully and effectively participating in the life of the body of Christ. If the ministers are the ones also to do the works of service and to build the body of Christ, what tasks would there be left for the rest of the saints? And, at what point would there be enough maturity on the part of the rest of the believers to begin to participate in the life of the body of Christ? If the rest of the saints were to function in any way in the body of Christ, how would they have to relate with the ministers? It is unlikely that Paul would have meant that the ministers Christ gave to the church were intended to be the only ones directly to work to the accomplishment of this ultimate goal.

---

6. For example, Best, *Critical and Exegetical*, 255.

Meaning and Imperative of Christian Spiritual Maturity

4.2.4   The Sequence Proposition of the Three Clauses

In the sequence proposition, the clause "for the equipment of the saints" is linked with "he gave"; "for the work of the ministry" is taken to be subordinate to "the equipment of the saints"; and the phrase "for building up the body of Christ" is understood as dependent on both the phrase "for the equipment of the saints" and the phrase "for the work of the ministry" together. Such understanding would mean that Christ gave to the church the ministers to equip the saints, so that the saints effectively exercise their gifts in service, so that by means of both the officers and the common service of the believers the body of Christ would be built. In line with this view, O'Brien argues that there is a movement of discussion from the work of the ministers (4:11) to that of the saints (4:12a, 12c).[7] From this view, ultimately the whole body grows from the head, as each part does its work (4:16), as the ministers listed in 4:11 supposedly support and direct other members of the church to carry out their several ministries for the good of the whole.

From this proposition, it would follow that the building up of the body of Christ would continue "until we all attain the unity of faith and of the knowledge of the Son of God, to mature man, to the measure of the stature of the fullness of Christ." This would make possible a relationship between what the ministers and the believers do as well as the building up of the body of Christ, with "until we all attain the unity of faith and of the knowledge of the Son of God, to the mature man, to the measure of the stature of the fullness of Christ" either as part of the stated goal or as simply a consequent byproduct of the process. There is no clarity as to whether "until we all attain the unity of faith and of the knowledge of the Son of God, to the mature man, to the measure of the stature of the fullness of Christ" is culmination of the building up of the body of Christ or an ultimate stage of the objective of the "equipping the saints."

4.2.5   The Mixed Proposition of the Three Clauses

In the mixed proposition, it is posited that the punctuation between "for the equipment of the saints" and "for the work of the ministry" be removed, so that the two clauses are in fact one clause with one idea: "for the equipment of the saints for the work of the ministry." The implication here then would be that "for the work of the ministry" is the objective of the ministers'

---

7. O'Brien, *Epistle*, 302.

work in "bringing the saints to completion." That means the sole purpose of equipping the saints would be for the saints to be capable of, as well as accustomed to, doing the works of service. This is seen not only as necessary but also as the methodology for "building up of the body of Christ." It would then follow that in carrying out the works of service the saints play their part in building up the body of Christ. This means the building up of the body of Christ is not a direct responsibility of the ministers. In support of this view, appeal is made to the change in preposition from πρὸς to εἰς between the first and second phrases, as a sign that the phrases are not coordinate to 4:7.

This proposition too is untenable because, as others have argued,[8] the change of preposition cannot bear the weight of such an argument, and there are in fact no grammatical or linguistic grounds for making a specific link between the first and second phrases. It is also argued that, although it is grammatically correct to combine "for the equipment of the saints" and "for the works of service," which would mean the whole community is to do the works of service, such a combination would render the clause "for building up the body of Christ" ambiguous—either intended to explain what "the works of service" means as the activity of all saints, or to explain what "for the equipment of the saints" means as the activity of the church leaders.

4.2.6 Alternative Proposition to the Three Clauses

The meaning of the clause "for the equipment of the saints" is pertinent to understanding its relationship with "for the works of service" and "for building up the body of Christ" and, ultimately, "until we all attain to the unity of faith and of the knowledge of the Son of God, to be mature man, to the measure of the stature of the fullness of Christ."

The meaning range of καταρτισμός includes preparing, completing, training and disciplining, with a view to making the trainee adequate for a specific task or general responsibility. Thus, if it stands alone, the phrase could mean to readmit lapsed saints into fellowship. Or, it could mean "to equip the saints," to make the saints holy and blameless. I would agree that the notion of making complete, through restoring or training, best fits the context. Thus, from the context of 4:7–12, Christ *intended* that all believers are brought to a state of completion, which would then imply that the saints are equipped for some purpose—the "works of service." Christ appointed

---

8. See Lincoln, *Ephesians*, 253; Muddiman, *Commentary*, 200.

the ministers for the purpose of making God's people fully qualified, so that what has been done for the saints, by the ministers and by the saints through the exercise of the gifts in service, is for (the continuous act of) building up the body of Christ. The process of equipping the saints, the execution of the works of service by the saints, and the continuous resultant progression towards the attainment of the goal of building the body of Christ will have to continue "until we all attain the unity of the faith and of the knowledge of the Son of God, to the mature man, to the measure of the stature of the fullness of Christ" (4:13). Although the building up of the body of Christ is the task of all members of the body (4:16), the ministers have a distinctive and particularly significant role to play in it: they must equip the members of the body so that they can fulfill their task.

As the saints presumably respond to the equipping process and increasingly put to use their gifts, the body of Christ is being built up. There is a direct purpose of Christ in appointing the ministers: to equip the saints for works of service. The ultimate intended result reflects the content and the specific objectives of the equipping process. Thus, Christ appointed ministers so that the ministry continues, until the church reaches the goal of maturity stated in 4:13.

4.3 Analysis and Interpretation of 4:13

μέχρι καταντήσωμεν οἱ πάντες εἰς τὴν ἑνότητα τῆς πίστεως καὶ τῆς ἐπιγνώσεως τοῦ υἱοῦ τοῦ θεοῦ, εἰς ἄνδρα τέλειον, εἰς μέτρον ἡλικίας τοῦ πληρώματος τοῦ Χριστοῦ

"Till we all come in the unity of the faith, and of the knowledge of the Son of God, unto a perfect man, unto the measure of the stature of the fullness of Christ."

4.3.1 Till We All Come

The literal sense of the verb, "till we all come" is until we all arrive at a place, thus it is primarily a temporal indicator. However, the verb also connotes intentionality to pursue the attainment of a specific state. Thus, μέχρι, "till," has both a prospective force and intentionality; the ministers are to *continue* to carry out their task both *until* the whole church reaches the particular destination stated and *in order that* the church might reach that destination. In using the word μέχρι Paul depicts the church as being, or expected to be, on the way to some specific final spiritual state. The church is to move towards the stated goal and keep moving until she attains that destination.

The inclusive "all" (οἱ πάντες) is part of the goal towards which "all" are to strive until they attain it. Since Paul is writing within the context of the church, the "all" here would refer only to the body of Christ, and not to the totality of all nations in all parts of the world. Because of the mention of apostles and evangelists in 4:11, numerical growth is probably also implied. However, introduction of the body metaphor implies the notion of the development of the church as an organism from within, through edification. It should be noted that Paul uses "we all" and not "each one of us," to counter possible over-individualization as well as underscore the corporate sense of spiritual maturity. Furthermore, the expression "may be built" implies a corporate rather than an individualistic view of spiritual maturity. Although the verb καταντάω generally means "to meet against, arrive, attain, come, and arriving completely at," in this context it refers to attaining or arriving at a *particular* final discernible point, state, or destination.

4.3.2 Unity of the Faith, and of the Knowledge of the Son of God

One of the elements of the final destination of the church is that the church grows towards unity of the faith and of the knowledge of the Son of God. This is unity of a particular kind, and one that is to be attained. There may be other kinds of unity, but in the end the church is to attain unity of faith and of the knowledge of the Son of God. Since faith and knowledge are not equivalent, the rendition would not be unity of faith that is the knowledge of the Son of God. Faith is not mere cognition, which knowledge is, but recognition, that is, comprehending all the elements of that state of mind of which the Son of God is the object, including the apprehension of his glory, the appropriation of his love, and confidence in and devotion to him.

From the construction of εἰς τὴν ἑνότητα τῆς πίστεως καὶ τῆς ἐπιγνώσεως τοῦ υἱοῦ τοῦ θεοῦ, it is clear that unity here is not the unity between faith and knowledge. Rather, it is the unity of faith *and* the unity of the knowledge of the Son of God—two distinct kinds of unity. The expression τοῦ υἱοῦ τοῦ θεοῦ suggests that the Son of God is the *only* object of knowledge, because of the article "the."

The "one faith" in 4:6, which Christians already have, is not the same as the unity of faith in 4:13. "One faith" may simply mean one creed, one confession of faith, independent of whether or not it has been accepted. There is "one faith." "Unity of faith" here does not refer to unity created by faith or resulting from common faith, not even to unity as that which lies in faith, as Best suggests.[9] Faith ranges in meaning between expressing the response to what God has done and the objective content of what is believed. The association of faith and knowledge, as well as the role of instruction and references to steadfastness in the face of false teaching, suggest that Paul has in mind faith as objective content, or the objective truths that the person has been taught and knowledge of this body of truths. Thus, "faith" in the context of 4:13 refers to a body of doctrine.

Because "unity of faith" is in relation to the destination of all Christians, then all Christians are to strive towards beholding to the same body of doctrine,[10] in a similar or common fashion. This would include holding to the same credal convictions[11] even if including the knowledge of the Son of God, but the context does not limit or even suggest that unity of faith is to be unity of faith in terms of only what Christians know and accept about the Son of God. There is "one faith" but the goal of Christian endeavor is unity of this faith, to fully appropriate the oneness of faith. The idea here is of the whole church moving towards the appropriation of all that is contained in its one faith. Thus, Christians are to continuously mature until they are all found to share a single faith and acknowledge a common bond.

---

9. See Best, *Critical and Exegetical*, 400.

10. Objectively, faith denotes that which is believed or that to which assent and affirmation are given. Subjectively, faith refers to the disposition to believe, assent, or affirm, or to the act of believing or affirming. In the New Testament, all uses of "faith" ultimately have to do with Jesus Christ. The principal areas reflected in relation to Jesus Christ as aspects of faith are: his unique kinship with God the Father (Matt 16:13–20), his person and work as the fulfillment of scriptural promises of a Messiah and a messianic kingdom (Matt 11–2–6), his power over nature and over evil (Luke 8:26–39), his moral and spiritual lordship over humankind through his teachings, his person, and his atoning work on the cross (Matt 28:16–20), and the reality of redemption from sin and victory over death in and through him (1 Cor 15:12–28).

11. Similar to what would be called the "rule of faith" or "canon of truth," which really means the central points of Christian teaching as articulated by the apostles, namely, that Christ was killed, raised from the dead, and exalted; that these things happened in fulfilment of Old Testament prophecies and were attested by the witness of the apostles; that God now is offering salvation to those who believe and repent and are baptized; and that in the end Jesus Christ will be the judge of all.

The Mature Church

Several possibilities exist with regard to the meaning of "the unity of the knowledge of the Son of God." Obviously, "the knowledge of the Son of God" cannot be knowledge that the Son of God possesses or the knowledge the Son of God has of the church. "The knowledge of the Son of God" could refer to the content of the faith, not simply the knowledge about the Son of God. Thus, "the unity of the knowledge of the Son of God" would refer to the unified content of what is known about the Son of God. As such, attaining to the unity of the knowledge of the Son of God then means appropriating all that is involved in salvation through Christ and the full knowledge of what is given in him. The possibility exists of Christians possessing the knowledge of the Son of God in a variety of ways and degrees. Paul's teaching here is that Christians attain a "oneness" with regard to the knowledge of the Son of God they possess, both in the content of the knowledge and the manner in which they all together possess it. Unlike what Paul writes earlier, where such knowledge of the Son of God was viewed as a gift to be received by the recipients,[12] it is now viewed also as a goal to strive for and attain.

Although this is the only place in Ephesians where the title "Son of God" appears, it should not be construed to mean that there were divergent views about Christ's sonship that were troubling the recipients. In any case, there is nothing to suggest that Paul is attacking any inappropriate notions with regard to the sonship of Christ to God, since he says nothing about the nature of true knowledge (of the Son of God). "Knowledge" here refers to that which is known, or what may be known, about the Son of God, and complete knowledge of the Son of God should then mean the full comprehension of the exalted Son of God.[13] The unity of this knowledge then may require a progressive movement toward full appropriation of the knowledge of Christ, which will result in a personal and living relationship with Christ. The church is to strive to come to this knowledge, which would exclude all diversity. With the knowledge of the Son of God, or fully knowing the Son of God, it then becomes possible for the church to have stability in sound knowledge, ability to resist wrong influence, ability and orientation to distinguish truth from falsehood, and ability and readiness to follow the truth and reject wickedness.

---

12. See Eph 1:17–19; 3:16–19
13. Cf. Liefield, *Ephesians*, 108.

4.3.3 Unto a Perfect Man

The use of the word for "man," which is the masculine noun for a male person, ἀνήρ, rather than the inclusive ἄνθρωπος, "human being," should be noted. Since Paul uses ἄνθρωπος when he refers to Adam, that is, the human being without the sexual aspect,[14] his use of ἀνήρ must be seen as deliberate. Ἀνήρ is the adult male, a full-grown man, normally in the fullness of his powers. With regard to τέλειον, some[15] think that here it refers to age, rather than stature, supposedly because τέλειον in the preceding clause means "mature" or "adult," hence in reference to age rather than stature; and νήπιος in the following verse means a child, in terms of age, and not in terms of size. To others,[16] stature, rather than age, is preferred here for the imagery of "fullness," since fullness is supposedly more naturally suited to spatial categories. Τέλειον is also considered to have the nuance of "mature" rather than "perfect." Yet to others,[17] the meaning of τέλειον is to be generated from the "full stature of Christ," since the fully grown male is taller than a female and thus more suitable as a metaphor for spiritual stature, and so the mature manhood refers to the cosmic Christ.

Although τέλειον has this wide range of meanings, in this clearly ethical context, it seems to refer to maturity, completeness, and perfection. Therefore, since in the context of 4:13 τέλειον modifies ἀνήρ, it should be translated as the "perfect man" or "man who is complete" or "full-grown adult male," presuming of course that the full-grown adult male correspondingly reflects the desired attributes. It follows that when used of a man, τέλειον means an adult, one who has reached the end of one's process of development as a man; when used in reference to a Christian, τέλειον then would mean one who has reached the end of one's development as a Christian; and when used in reference to the church, it means the church has reached the end in her development and stands complete, that is, in complete conformity to Christ. Since Paul is writing in relation to the church, τέλειον here is in reference to the church. It means, therefore, that in its complete state the church is seen as a corporate entity, as "we all" are to move toward "the mature person," not "mature people" and as Robinson

---

14. See, for example, Eph 4:2,15, 4:22–24
15. For example, Hodge, *Commentary*, 234.
16. See, for example, O'Brien, *Epistle*, 308.
17. See Muddiman, *Commentary*, 204.

aptly puts it;[18] the plural is in the lower stage of Christian spiritual maturity only, if it is Christian spiritual maturity in the first place.

4.3.4 Unto the Measure of the Stature of the Fullness of Christ

The word "measure" (μέτρον) occurs in the Bible in a variety of renditions. In this context, "measure" may not refer to an instrument by means of which size or quantity is measured nor to a step or definite part of a progressive course or policy, a means to an end, or an act designed for the accomplishment of an object.[19] Since in this context μέτρον is a noun, it may not refer to ascertaining by use of a measuring instrument or to compute the extent, quantity, dimensions, or capacity of something. Here μέτρον will refer to being of a certain size or quantity, or to having a certain length, breadth, thickness, or intensity, or having certain capacity, according to a defined standard. Thus μέτρον here refers to a standard of dimension; a fixed unit of quantity or extent; an extent or quantity in the fractions or multiples of which anything is estimated and stated; hence, a rule by which anything is adjusted or judged. It also refers to the dimensions or capacity, size, or extent of something according to some standard.

Given the ambiguity of ἡλικία, its meaning must be determined from the context. Since the context contains the contrast between children and adults, ἡλικία could be validly interpreted as age, as a further part of this contrast and as an explanation of what was meant by "mature person." Age is favored by the general context because of the notion of maturity, since adults are more mature than children. The term νήπιοι in 4:14 would contrast favorably with the idea of maturity. But also filling and building are metaphors of space and from these the idea of size is appropriate, after μέτρον. From this discussion, it appears that ἡλικία is used with both age and size in mind and therefore its interpretation would require a consideration of both age and size. But age and size together constitute maturity (or immaturity for a young age and small size).

The πληρώματος of Christ is quite an ambiguous in 4:13. The πληρώματος of Christ can refer to that which fills him or that which he fills. The "measure of the stature of the fullness of Christ" may also be interpreted as the full measure of the complete stature, or maturity, of the

---

18. Robinson, *St. Paul's Epistle*, 101.
19. See "Measure" in *Encyclopaedia Britannica*.

Meaning and Imperative of Christian Spiritual Maturity

fulfilled Christ,[20] but this would raise serious theological questions such as whether there was a point in time when Christ was not fulfilled. The "fullness of Christ" could mean the "plenitude of excellence" that Christ possesses or that he bestows. Words related to πλήρωμα include the verb πληρόω ("I fill"), signifying that which is or has been filled, and also that which fills or with which a thing is filled; it would then signify "fullness" or "a fulfilling." That being the case, it would also refer to a state of being full, abundant, or complete. In the New Testament, outside the Gospels,[21] only Paul uses the term πλήρωμα, employing it twelve times, four of which are to be found in Ephesians.[22] Prior to 4:13, Paul writes, "unto a dispensation of the fullness of the times" (1:10), "which is his body, the fullness of him who fills everything in every way" (1:23),[23] and "that you may be filled to the measure of all the fullness of God" (3:19).

In Ephesians, Paul uses πλήρωμα sometimes with reference to Christ, as Christ is himself to "fulfill" all things in heaven and on earth,[24] and other times with reference to the church and the individual Christian. The "the fullness of Christ" in 4:13 is perhaps not to be separated from "the church, which is his body, the fullness of him who fills all in all" in Ephesians, meaning that Christ is being fulfilled, and finds his fullness in the church. In Colossians[25] "the fullness" of God in Christ is contrasted with the angelic powers that were supposedly intermediate between God and

20. See also Robinson, *St. Paul's Epistle*, 101.

21. The occurrences in the Gospels are in: Matt 9:16 and Mark 2:21, where it means "the fullness," that by which a gap or rent is filled up, as in patching a torn garment; Mark 6:43, saying "they took up fragments, the fullness of twelve baskets"; Mark 8:20, saying "the fullness of how many baskets of fragments did ye take up?"; and John 1:16, where it says "out of his fullness we all received."

22. Outside of Ephesians, Paul uses πλήρωμα in Rom 11:12, "If their loss (is) the riches of the Gentiles, how much more their fullness?"—"fullness" of Israel here referring to the nation of Israel being received by God for participation in all the benefits of Christ's salvation; Rom 11:25, "A hardening hath befallen Israel, until the fullness of the Gentiles come in"; Rom 13:10, "love is the fulfilment (the fulfilling) of the law," "fulfillment" meaning a complete filling up of what the law requires; Rom 15:29, "I shall come in the fullness of the blessing of Christ"; 1 Cor 10:26, "The earth is the Lord's, and the fullness thereof"; Gal 4:4, "when the fullness of the time came," meaning that portion of time by which the longer antecedent period is completed; Col 1:19, "In him should all the fullness dwell"; and Col 2:9, "For him the whole fullness of deity bodily" (RSV).

23. That means the church is the fullness of Christ—the body of believers filled with the presence, power, agency, and riches of Christ.

24. See Eph 4:10.

25. See Col 1:19; 2:9.

The Mature Church

the world. The false teachers at Colossae seem to have employed the term "fullness" to signify the entire series of angels, which filled the space and the interval between a holy God and the world of matter, which was conceived of as essentially and necessarily evil. In a contradistinction to the Colossian false teaching in regard to "the fullness," Paul shows that in Christ all the fullness of the Godhead dwells bodily.[26]

The "fullness of Christ" in the context of 4:13 therefore refers to the church attaining the standard or the level of a church that is filled with Christ, or that Christ fills, as well as the church attaining complete conformity to Christ, and all Christians reaching this high standard. The measure of the stature of the fullness of Christ means attaining the perfection of faith, and the essence of that is to hold fast to Christ as true and perfect God and to mature unto full understanding of the divinity of the Son of God. Since in this context πλήρωμα more naturally also has spatial connotations, the standard for the believers' attainment can be taken to be the mature proportions that befit the church as the fullness of Christ. As such, the church has by faith the full possession of all that Christ has to impart, particularly his moral, intellectual, and spiritual perfection.

One notes that 4:13 is a part of a sentence that continues to 4:16. Whereas 4:16 suggests that the goal is the complete growth of the body of Christ, each of the three phrases in 4:13 incorporates a reference to Christ involving an understanding of Christ and a relationship with him. Although the use of the word μέχρι suggests a time frame for the attainment of the goal, Paul does not in the text suggest when the goal will be or is expected to be attained. The full maturity to be attained is more specifically defined by its measure, namely, the full stature of Christ. The glorified Christ provides the standard at which his people are to aim—the perfection of the personal Christ. The clause "so that we may no longer be children . . ." provides a general comment on the current state of the readers, but also indicates what should take place if genuine progress towards the final destination is to be made. With the building up and bringing to completion of the church, immaturity and instability can increasingly be left behind, and the church will increasingly move into a mature state.

---

26. I suppose the fullness of the Godhead (Col 2:9; 3:19) is the totality of the divine powers and attributes as eternal, infinite, and unchangeable in existence, knowledge, wisdom, power, holiness, goodness, truth, and love. The fullness of the nature of God would be his life, light, and love, and this has its permanent dwelling in Christ. This implies that the fullness of Christ is the timeless and eternal inhabitation of the fullness of the Godhead from the Father to the Son.

Meaning and Imperative of Christian Spiritual Maturity

4.4 Meaning of Christian Spiritual Maturity

From the foregoing analysis, and therefore according to 4:13, Christian spiritual maturity means all Christians, together as the church, ultimately attaining a state of oneness of the contents of faith; acceptance and possession of a complete, correct, and full understanding of Christ; and being so completely filled with Christ's essence in his glorified state that the church, in full conformity with Christ, is an accurate, full, physical manifestation of Christ in the world. As such, Christian spiritual maturity has the following four dimensions:

- **Meaning and essence:** Christian spiritual maturity refers to a specific final and discernible destination, and arrival at that destination is supposed to be for all Christians, who increasingly become "one" as they approach that destination.

- **Means of attainment:** Christian spiritual maturity is a sequel of the ministry participation, variously, of all Christians as started off and continuously equipped and guided by the ministers Christ has appointed and has given as gifts to the church. All are to strive towards Christian spiritual maturity. Unlike salvation, which is by divine grace alone,[27] Christian spiritual maturity is a product of salvation, and it requires sustained human effort to attain it or to be moving towards the attainment of the same.

- **Point of attainment:** In theory, the point at which Christian spiritual maturity is attained is when the whole church has attained the goal. The church is to grow to become an appropriate body, befitting as well as worthy of the Head, Christ. Practically, however, as each time there is a new convert to the Christian faith who will need to be discipled, the configuration changes back to a state of spiritual immaturity, and as new believers continue to join the church, the duration of attaining the goal of ultimate Christian spiritual maturity is at consummation.

- **Indicators of progression towards Christian spiritual maturity:** Indicators of Christian spiritual maturity are an important dimension of Christian spiritual maturity. They include corporate stability and constancy in the truth, ability to discern error and reject or correct it, ability and predisposition to speak the truth in love, and meaningful participation of all members through effective use of their individual

27. See Eph 2:8–10; cf. Rom 3:21–30.

gifts. Unity is a reality that occurs by default when there is Christian spiritual maturity. That means maturity will bring about unity, but not the other way round.

4.5 The Imperative of Christian Spiritual Maturity

A key question may arise from the identified meaning of Christian spiritual maturity. Is Christian spiritual maturity just something nice, good, or important, or is it necessary? Is Paul merely recommending to the church, or inviting the church, to consider and make a decision whether or not to grow towards such Christian spiritual maturity? This section examines the implications of the meaning of Christian spiritual maturity within the context of 4:13–16.

4.5.1 Lack of Christian Spiritual Maturity Is Dangerous for Christians

It is apparent that Christian spiritual maturity is imperative, as without it Christians will not stop being "infants." The "so that" preceding "we will be no longer children" (4:14) shows the consequences related to lack of Christian spiritual maturity. The weight of the use of "children" imagery and its elaboration suggests a call for the church to grow towards full Christian spiritual maturity, or risk being in grave danger. In this context, being an infant is a negative image.[28] The harsh reality of being in that state is compared to a ship without a rudder and thus helplessly tossed to and fro by the waves and driven about by every wind.

Thus, spiritually immature Christians, like children, will be volatile in their beliefs, unstable, foolish, and incapable of understanding the truth. The contrast between "mature manhood" in 4:13 and the term "children" in 4:14 suggests that the ignorance and instability of "children" stand in contradistinction to the knowledge of the mature adult. The term used, κλυδωνιζόμενοι, suggests rough waters, and the passive participle of the

---

28. Νήπιοι could be used positively, to symbolize simplicity and innocence, cleanness from adult decadence (see, for example, 1 Pet 2:2; Matt 11:25; 18:3; 21:16; Luke 10:21). Negatively, as is the case in this context, children are pictured as unstable, lacking in direction, susceptible to deception, and open to manipulation. This is being *childish*. God is pleased with the *child-like*, the innocent ones. Therefore, a distinction is to be made between being child-like and being childish.

Meaning and Imperative of Christian Spiritual Maturity

cognate verb means tossed by waves, the same term used in Luke 8:24 and James 1:6. So the picture here is that an immature church, which will actually be immature individual Christians, will be entirely at the mercy of the waves and the wind—which know no mercy. Also, the state of confusion and lack of direction contrast strongly with the goal-oriented language of 4:13. The implications here are that the immature Christians are endangered and are prone to the perversion of false instruction, with adverse repercussions for faith living. This means that immaturity on the part of Christians cannot be treated as a neutral state that will be outgrown in due course. It is a highly dangerous state because it lays Christians open to manipulation by cunning persons and forces of error and makes them easy prey to false teachings. In the context of 4:13, therefore, Christian spiritual maturity is necessary. On the one hand, lack of Christian spiritual maturity will mean the recipients individually remaining children, unable to discern and reject or oppose dangerous false teachings. On the other hand, it is implied that only with such Christian spiritual maturity will Christians no longer possess or display the negative characteristics of being children.

4.5.2 False Teachers, and Their False Teachings and Methods Are Difficult to Discern and Resist

The description Paul gives of false teaching, false teachers and the methods the false teachers use also reflects the imperative of spiritual maturity. In the context of 4:14, Christians can expect to face false teachings. "Every wind of doctrine" suggests different kinds of teaching that stand over against the unity of faith and knowledge to which the recipients are to attain. It is likely that these different kinds of teachings would include the various religious philosophies that threatened to undermine the gospel, not just the teaching within the church.[29] Because Paul does not give specifics of "every wind

---

29. Best (*Critical and Exegetical*, 405) suggests that as Christians were under continual pressure from other Christians in respect of what was true teaching, each teacher claiming truth in what he was teaching, and that because a variety of teaching and doctrinal novelty would have been normal during this stage of the church, Paul would in this regard be referring to the variety of teaching within the church rather than false philosophies and theologies entering it from outside. This view is, however, debatable because it fails to take cognizance of the force of the adjective "every" in the phrase "every wind of teaching," which suggests any and all kinds of teaching. It is better, therefore, to take this as a reference to the false teaching in the guise of the various religious philosophies that threatened to assimilate, and thereby dilute or undermine the gospel, both from within and from outside the church.

of doctrine" (παντὶ ἀνέμῳ τῆς διδασκαλίας), it may suggest that he is talking about the general dangers that were a hindrance to those not firmly grounded in the faith. Unable to come to settled convictions or to evaluate various forms of teaching, immature Christians would fall easy prey to every new theological fashion or trend.

That the false teachers are intentional and ready to do everything possible to deceive and mislead signifies the malicious deception by which the false teachers seek to lead the unstable astray. In the metaphor of the sea and its storms, false teachings are described as having the potential to destroy, derail, or uproot. The singular διδασκαλίας with the definite article implies a specific false Christian teaching, but the qualification παντὶ with ἀνέμῳ indicates a variety of winds and therefore a variety of teachings. Since the remainder of the epistle is largely devoted to ethical instruction, the false teaching may also be about behavior, over and above heretical doctrinal teaching.

Paul attributes departure from the truth to the false teachers, who are by methodology and tendency, cunning, and deceitful. That means false teachers are not simply uninformed or incorrect teachers, and therefore false teachers can never be innocent. In the phrase ἐν τῇ κυβείᾳ τῶν ἀνθρώπων, ἐν πανουργίᾳ πρὸς τὴν μεθοδείαν, Paul uses the term κυβεία ("cunning") and the preposition πρὸς ("according to"), which show that he is talking about cunning according to the craft that error uses. It is the same word used to describe the Serpent's act when he deceived Eve in the garden.[30] Satan's machinations have a method; his aim is to mislead. Thus, behind the false teaching are not simply evil men and women who pursue their unscrupulous goals with a scheming that produces error (πλάνη, deceit, false teaching), standing against apostolic practice and the truth. Rather, behind the false teacher is a supernatural evil power that seeks to deceive Christians.

The expression ἐν τῇ κυβείᾳ τῶν ἀνθρώπων indicates the direction of tendency, that, this cunning is designed to seduce. The term μεθοδείαν occurs only in 4:14 (and 6:11, where it is in plural, μεθοδείας, referring to the wiles of the devil) and can be defined as the "well-thought-out, methodical art of leading astray"[31] or human trickery.[32] The term is derived from

---

30. See 2 Cor 11:3; Gen 3:1–9.

31. Cf. Lincoln, *Ephesians*, 259; Best, *Critical and Exegetical*, 406; Muddiman, *Commentary*, 207.

32. See Hendriksen, *Ephesians*, 202.

μεθοδεύω, which essentially means to track a person down, as a wild animal would its prey. Francis Foulkes[33] captures the broader notion of the "tossing winds," where, in Paul's mind, the false doctrines constitute a general evil atmosphere where current wrong doctrines exert their force on the Christians. Ephesians 4:14 shows that the ministry was given not only to enable the church to grow but also so that the church would be able to resist any forces that might attempt to corrupt or destroy it. What this means is that Christian spiritual maturity is simply a must for the church.

4.6 Conclusion

In Ephesians 4:13–16, Paul presents spiritual maturity as both central to and imperative for the life and witness of the church. In her new identity (chs. 1–3) the church needs spiritual maturity (4:13–16) in order to live in accordance with the new morality commensurate with the new identity (4:17—6:20). In interpreting 4:13–16, the meaning of Christian spiritual maturity has been determined. Christian spiritual maturity refers to a specific final and discernible destination of all Christians, who increasingly become "one" as they approach that destination. All Christians are to strive towards Christian spiritual maturity. Therefore, unlike salvation, which is by divine grace alone, Christian spiritual maturity is a product of salvation that requires sustained human effort to be moving towards the goal. Although in theory the point at which Christian spiritual maturity is attained is when the whole church reaches the destination, practically, as each time there is a new convert to the Christian faith who will need to be discipled, the configuration changes back to a state of spiritual immaturity. This means that as new believers continue to join the church, the ultimate Christian spiritual maturity will be realized at consummation.

Analysis and interpretation has also shown that Christian spiritual maturity is imperative for the church, because without such maturity the church will fall prey to false and wrong doctrinal teachings, taught by persons from within and from outside the church who are both intentional about and highly skilful in scheming to lead Christians into error.

Two implications of the meaning and imperative of Christian spiritual maturity are apparent. First, since Christian spiritual maturity is the ultimate goal of the church, and if the essence and life of the Christian faith is the primary focus of the New Testament, the church needs to be intentional

---

33. Foulkes, *Ephesians*, 350.

The Mature Church

and systematic in developing and implementing authentic programs towards spiritual maturity. The leadership of the church in general needs itself to be in the process of striving towards Christian spiritual maturity. It is obvious that a church organized and administered by leaders who lack Christian spiritual maturity can only be a church of largely spiritually immature members.

And second, Christian spiritual maturity must form an important part of the modern-day evangelical Christian scholarship agenda. In a time of religious fundamentalism, even discussion of Christian spiritual maturity may be viewed with disdain. It might appear as if the goal is to promote fundamentalism of another kind. This need not be the case. In fact, this is all the more reason why evangelical Christian scholars would want to bring the subject of Christian spiritual maturity into their academic agenda. As such, among other things, more research is needed in the area of Christian spiritual maturity to inform concerted efforts to continue building up Christians so that they can be "the "salt of the earth" and "the light of the world."[34]

---

34. See Matt 5:13–14. Spiritually mature Christians will then be able to influence society, as expected, to make the earth a better and wholesome place, much as salt purifies, preserves, heals, and enhances the flavor of food. Similarly, spiritually mature Christians, as light of the world, will be able to illuminate and give guidance to society, which is in darkness.

5

Spiritual Maturity in the Church: A Case Study

5.1 Introduction

A basic research project was conducted to determine the understanding and level of spiritual maturity of the church in a specific context and compare them with the meaning of spiritual maturity according to Ephesians 4:1–13. What was needed, therefore, was a descriptive survey[1] of the population or a sample, in terms of the dimensions of spiritual maturity, rather than a gathering of expert opinions to building the understanding of spiritual maturity. The Anglican Diocese of Mount Kilimanjaro, Tanzania, was selected as a convenience sample (see Bailey 1987:93); and the individual respondents were selected purposively[2]. A self-administered questionnaire was developed in English, translated into Kiswahili, pre-tested and distributed to all parishes in Arusha, Babati and Kilimanjaro Deaneries[3]

1. In essence, a descriptive survey looks at the population or the sample thereof, and describes it. The method entails looking at or observing accurately a phenomenon and describing it as accurately as possible (see Leedy, *Practical Research*, 133–34). A questionnaire is often a necessary tool of observation, to collect the baseline data of the respondents in terms of their demographics (age, occupation, marital status, educational levels, and roles and responsibilities) and their psychographics (attitudes, knowledge, opinions, practices, and views). Surveys are generally effective and can be cross-sectional studies, panel studies, or trend studies (see Shoemaker & McCombs, "Survey Research," 150–52). For further discussion on the critical considerations to make in questionnaire construction and administration, see Trochim, *Research Methods*, 108ff.).

2. See Bailey, *Methods*; and Trochim, *Research Methods*; 56). The focus of the study was the leadership of the church, and so the criterion for selection is all people in leadership positions at congregation level.

3. In Anglican church polity, a diocese is a jurisdiction under a bishop. A diocese

The Mature Church

that could be reached, with appropriate instructions in Kiswahili to the pastors. The questionnaire contained both closed questions and open-ended questions.[4] The questionnaire was distributed to all leaders in each church, which included, as applicable in each church, the pastor, the pastor's wife (if any), the Parish Council members,[5] the chairperson and secretary of the Mothers Union, the chairperson and secretary of the youth organization, and the leaders of the choirs. It was assumed such leaders existed but it was not known exactly which ones exist in each congregation or how many they are. This chapter presents the results of the data analysis and an interpretation as well as a discussion of the findings.

5.2 Analysis of Data and Interpretation of Findings

A total of 250 questionnaires were sent to the churches, of which 81 completed questionnaires were returned. Two questionnaires were too incomplete to be useful and were therefore discarded, hence, 79 questionnaires were used for the data analysis stage.[6] The responses to the open-ended questions were analyzed and the recurring responses were coded and made part of the complete codebook for the entire questionnaire. Using the Statistical Package for Social Scientists (SPSS),[7] the data entry was performed data entry clerk, after which the data was analyzed in terms of frequency distributions.

---

would usually be divided into deaneries, each led by a dean. Whereas a diocese would consist of 2–25 deaneries, a deanery would normally comprise of 3–5 parishes, depending on the number of the members, geographical access to those members, and the economic ability or potential of the deaneries to sustain themselves financially and administratively. A parish, which is usually administered by a parish priest or vicar, may have more than one congregation. Each parish as well as each congregation would have leadership, appointed or elected.

4. Closed questions are items with a complete list of options with appropriate instructions for the respective respondents to select whichever is applicable to them, and open-ended questions are items in which space is provided for the respondents to write the answers and thus respond in any way they wish (see Newell, "Questionnaires.", 101–2).

5. Parish council members are also known as church elders. Where the congregation is part of a parish, they are only referred to as church elders. However, whether they are parish council members or church elders, their role and responsibilities as well as their status are practically the same.

6. This was a 32% questionnaire return rate. However, given the fact that the questionnaires sent out may have been too many for the number of leaders available, this return rate is considered acceptable.

7. There are other comparable statistical analysis packages, such as SAS, Minitab, P-Stat, and Systat (See Procter, "Analysing Survey Data," 240). The SPSS was used because

Spiritual Maturity in the Church: A Case Study

In the analysis of the data, two-thirds (67%) of the respondents were male, and 33% female. This means that there were twice as many men as women in the leadership composition of the church. Very few respondents (2.6%) were below 21 years of age, and 12.8% were above 50 years of age. The vast majority of the respondents (84.6%) were between 21 and 50 years of age. A large majority (81%) of the respondents were married, about one in eight (12%) had never married, and one in twenty respondents (5%) had separated from their spouses.

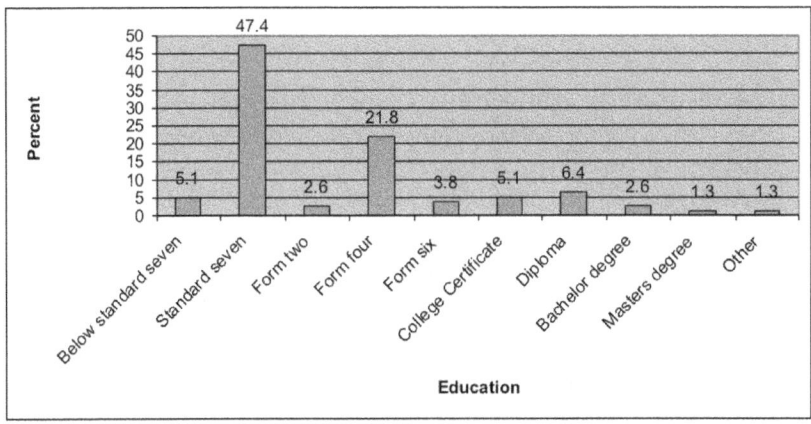

Figure 5.1: Highest Educational Levels of the Respondents

As Figure 5.1 shows, nearly a half (47.4%) of the respondents had primary-level education, 21.8% had Form Four–level education, and 3.8% had Form Six–level education. Only 15.4% of the respondents had education level higher than Form Six, such as a college certificate (5.1%), a diploma (6.4%), a bachelors degree (2.6%), or a masters degree (1.3%). It is interesting to note that some church leaders (5.1%) had education lower than primary level.

A half of the respondents (50%) were small-scale farmers or were involved in small-scale animal husbandry. Nearly one in six (15.4%) were employed mainly as school or kindergarten teacher, accounting clerks, secretaries, or were in the military. About one in ten (10.3%) were involved in small business or petty trading, and nearly 27% had some other occupation, such as students or housewives, or did not specify their primary occupation.

---

of its availability and its strength for purposes of the study. Norusis (*SPSS Guide* and SPSS/PC+) provides an excellent guide on SPSS.

The Mature Church

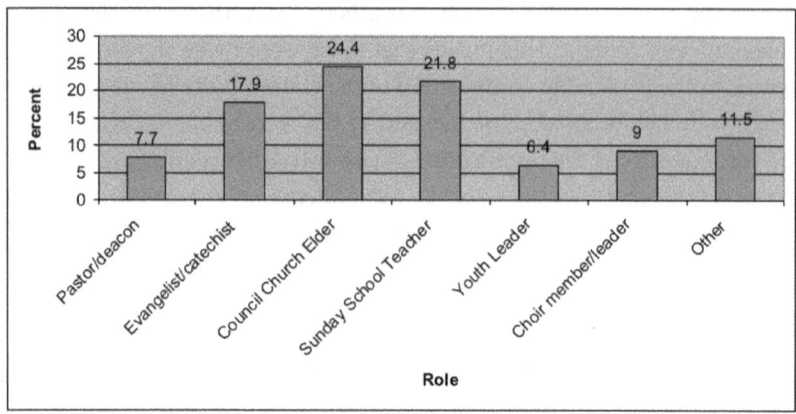

Figure 5.2: Respondent's Role in the Church

As Figure 5.2 indicates, the respondents were pastors (7.7%), evangelists or catechists (17.9%), church council members (24.4%), Sunday school teachers (21.8%), youth leaders (6.4%), choir leaders (9%), and in other leadership roles, including leaders of the Mothers' Union and church administrators (11.5%). One respondent (1.3%) did not indicate church responsibility. Thus, as the study intended, all respondents were leaders in the church.

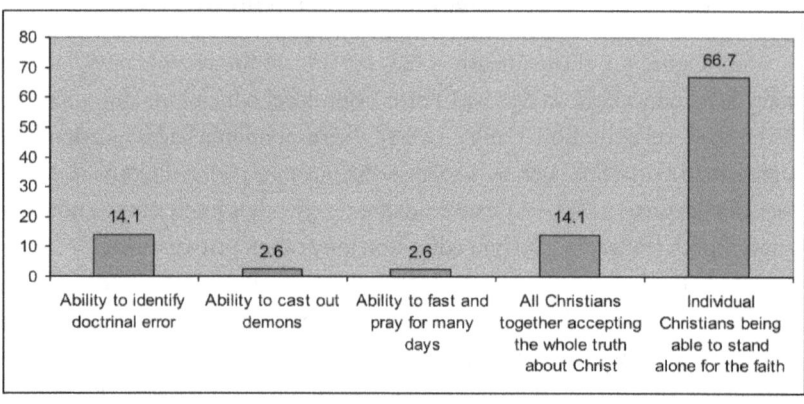

Figure 5.3: Statement that Describes Spiritual Maturity Most Accurately according to the Respondents

The results of the statement that describes spiritual maturity most accurately are shown in Figure 5.3. It was found that two-thirds (67%) of the respondents chose "individual Christians being able to stand alone for the faith," 14% chose "ability to identify doctrinal error," 14% chose "all

Spiritual Maturity in the Church: A Case Study

Christians together accepting the whole truth about Christ." Very few (2.6%) chose "ability to cast out demons" or "ability to fast and pray for many days."

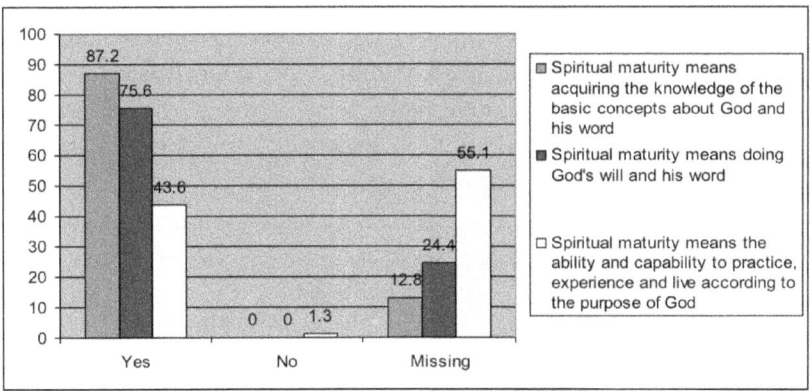

Figure 5.4: The Meaning of Spiritual Maturity according to the Respondents

Figure 5.4 shows the respondents' understanding of the meaning of spiritual maturity. The vast majority (87.2%) of the respondents indicated that spiritual maturity means acquiring knowledge of the basic concepts about God and his word; three in four (75.6%) indicated that spiritual maturity means doing God's will and his word; 43.6% indicated that spiritual maturity means an individual Christian's ability and capability to practice, experience, and live according to the purpose of God. The "missing" scores in Figure 5.4 are computer-generated and in this case indicate, in percentage, the number of respondents who did not mention that particular option.

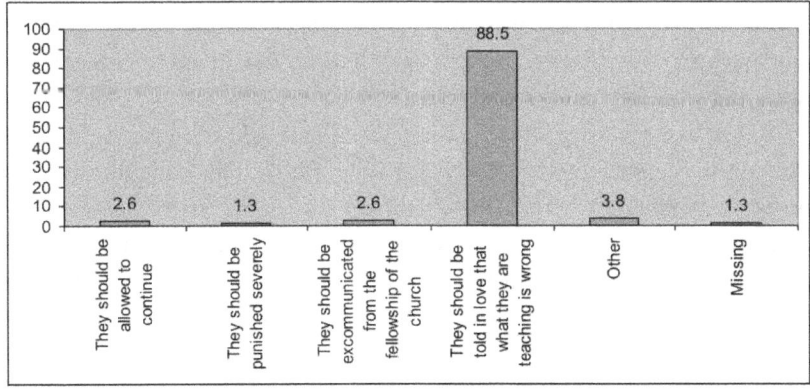

Figure 5.5: What Is to Be Done to People Who Teach Wrong Doctrines in the Church?

101

The Mature Church

With regard to "What is to be done to people who teach wrong doctrines in the church?" (Figure 5.5), the vast majority (88.5%) said that such people should be told in love that what they are teaching is wrong. It is interesting to note that some (2.6%) said that such people should be allowed to continue or should be excommunicated, and half as many (1.3%) said such people should be punished severely. The "missing" scores are a computer-generated reflection of the percentage of respondents who did not mention the respective course of action.

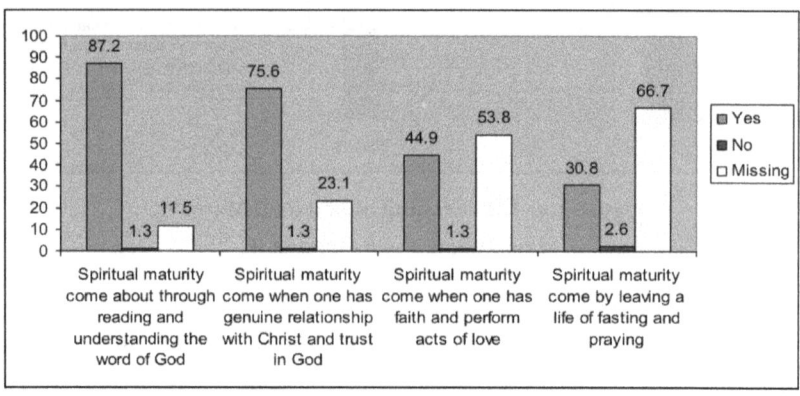

Figure 5.6: How Spiritual Maturity Comes About according to the Respondents

As Figure 5.6 shows[8], the vast majority (87%) of the respondents said spiritual maturity comes about through reading and understanding the Bible. More than three quarters of the respondents (76%) also said spiritual maturity comes about when one has a genuine relationship with Christ and trusts in God, 45% said spiritual maturity comes about when one has faith and performs acts of love, and 31% said that spiritual maturity comes about by living a life of fasting and praying.

The vast majority (87%) of the respondents said an important indicator of the presence of spiritual maturity in the church is the transformed lives of members, whereby the members also demonstrate accurate understanding of the Bible. About two-thirds (65.4%) said that an important indicator of spiritual maturity is faithful attendance and participation in church activities such as prayer events, evangelism and outreach Programs.

8. The question provided opportunity for the respondents to write more than one response. Because of the multiple responses from the respondents, the percentages are not to be added up. Thus, these percentages reflect the relative weights of preference of the various courses of action.

Nearly as many (64%) also said an important indicator of the presence of spiritual maturity in the church is church growth through increased membership. About four in ten (38.5%) respondents said an important indicator of spiritual maturity is giving for the work of God.

About six in ten (61.5%) of the respondents said spiritual maturity becomes complete when people change and accept Christ as their Lord and Savior. About half (52.6%) said spiritual maturity becomes complete when church members correctly understand and keep the word of God, or when there is correct teaching and understanding of the Bible (35.9%). One-third (33.3%) said that spiritual maturity would become complete when Christ returns, or when the church overcomes temptations (11.5%), and almost one in ten (9%) said that spiritual maturity will never become complete in this life.

The vast majority (88.5%) said that spiritual maturity is important for serving God fully. Nearly seven in ten (69%) said that spiritual maturity is important for understanding the Bible, nearly two-thirds (64%) said spiritual maturity is important for building the body of Christ, about one third (32%) said spiritual maturity is important for Christians to overcome temptations, and nearly one-fourth (23%) said spiritual maturity is important for the manifestations of God's deeds, such as miracles.

The vast majority of the respondents (83.3%) said unity demonstrates love, three quarters (74.4%) also said unity manifests spiritual maturity, 56.4% said spiritual maturity and love are the result of knowing God, and 15.4% said spiritual maturity and love together allow members to exercise the gifts of the Holy Spirit. Furthermore, about nine in ten respondents (89.7%) understood love to be a fruit of spiritual maturity, as three in four (76%) understood that without spiritual maturity there is no love. Some (13%) understood that whereas spiritual maturity is about knowing God, love is about loving people. These results suggest an understanding among the respondents that not only is love a fruit of spiritual maturity but also that spiritual maturity is the source of love.

Nearly nine in ten respondents (87%) would respond to erroneous teaching by a leader in the church by explaining to the person the truth in love, eight in ten (80%) would respond to the erroneous teaching by stopping the person, and seven in ten (68%) would respond to erroneous teaching by praying for and warning the person. A few (3.8%) said they would abandon a church leader teaching erroneous teachings and follow other leaders or keep quiet and do nothing, in order to avoid triggering a conflict (2.6%).

Three key points the respondents learned from Ephesians 4:13 were that the church needs unity of faith and love (91%), knowing and growing in Christ makes Christians complete (89%), spiritual maturity leads to fullness of Christ (83%), and the need or importance of having faith, love, patience, and holiness (54%).

The vast majority (90%) of the respondents strongly agreed that spiritual maturity is not just good but is necessary for the church, and 5% others agreed. Interestingly, some (1.3%) strongly disagreed with the statement and others (1.3%) were neutral. These results show that, largely, spiritual maturity was understood as necessary for the church, and not just a good thing.

The majority (74%) of the respondents agreed, nearly half of them (36%) strongly, that spiritual maturity means that all the members of the church understand all the fundamental teachings about Christ the same way; 9% were neutral and nearly 14% disagreed, including 10% who strongly disagreed. This means that although there is generally an understanding that spiritual maturity means all members understand the fundamental teachings about Christ the same way, there was a significant percentage of respondents (23%) who did not hold this view, and almost half of those strongly disagreed. This implies diversity of understanding of the meaning of spiritual maturity. Furthermore, 41% of the respondents strongly agreed and 37% others agreed that spiritual maturity means that all the members of the church accept all the fundamental teachings about Christ the same way, and nearly one in five (19%) disagreed, with nearly half of them (9%) strongly disagreeing with that view. A small minority (3.8%) were neutral on this matter.

Two-thirds (67%) of the respondents agreed, with most of them (54%) agreeing strongly, that when there is full spiritual maturity Christians will fiercely oppose other church members and church leaders who teach erroneous doctrines. About 14% strongly disagreed with this view, about 13% others disagreed, and 6.4% were neutral. These results show some diversity of views, but generally project a hostile predisposition towards erroneous, heretical, or false teachers.

Nearly three quarters (73%) of the respondents strongly disagreed with the view that where the church is spiritually mature, its members will tolerate doctrinal error and take no action about it, and 6.4% others disagreed. Surprisingly, nearly 12% of them agreed with this view, with some of them (2.6%) even agreeing strongly. Thus, generally, the respondents would not tolerate doctrinal error.

One in four (26%) respondents strongly agreed and about 27% others agreed that the primary means towards attaining spiritual maturity are baptism and confirmation. One-fifth (20.5%) of the respondents strongly disagreed and 17% disagreed with this view. One in ten (10.3%) respondents were neutral about it. These results show a split among the respondents, with just over a half (53%) understanding baptism and confirmation to be the primary means towards spiritual maturity, and the remaining 48% not agreeing, and even strongly disagreeing, that baptism and confirmation are the primary means of spiritual maturity.

Nearly half (47%) of the respondents strongly agreed that accepting Christ as Lord and Savior would normally follow after one attains some spiritual maturity, and nearly a third as many (15%) agreed with that view. One-fifth (20.5%) of the respondents strongly disagreed and 3.8% others disagreed with the view that accepting Christ as Lord and Savior would normally follow after one attains some spiritual maturity. Very few (2.6%) were neutral about this view. Also, nearly all respondents (99%) strongly agreed with the view that in order for the church to grow towards spiritual maturity, correct and systematic biblical teaching is necessary.

Most respondents strongly agreed (63%) or agreed (23%) with the view that the focus on bringing about spiritual maturity has to be more on the corporate life of the church and less upon individual Christians. Some respondents, however, strongly disagreed (7.7%) or disagreed (5%) with this view, and very few (1.3%) were neutral about the view.

More than two-thirds of the respondents did not agree with the view that spiritual maturity is a good thing but is not all that necessary to grow to spiritual maturity. In this regard, 63% strongly disagreed and 15.4% disagreed. Surprisingly, one in five (20.6%) respondents strongly agreed (10.3%) or agreed (10.3%) that spiritual maturity is a good thing but not all that necessary to grow to spiritual maturity, and 1.3% were neutral.

More than a half (53%) of the respondents strongly agreed with the view that, unlike salvation, spiritual maturity requires human effort to attain, and 7.7% agreed with it. However, nearly 22% strongly disagreed, 13% others disagreed, and 3.8% were neutral. From these results, it appears that although six in ten (60.3%) recognized the necessity of human effort in attaining spiritual maturity, nearly 35% of them denied any necessity of human effort to contribute towards the attainment of spiritual maturity. Similarly, the majority of the respondents either strongly disagreed (41%) or disagreed (15%) with the view that, like salvation, spiritual maturity does not require human effort to attain it. Surprisingly, however, many strongly agreed (22%) or agreed (14%) with the view, and 7.7% were neutral about it.

The majority (69%) of the respondents strongly disagreed (54%) or disagreed (15%) with the view that it is acceptable for the church to win unbelievers by any means, including deceiving and luring them so that by any means they get them into the kingdom of God. Surprisingly, however, one in four (26%) respondents strongly agreed (14%) or agreed (12%) with the view, and 3.8% were neutral. These results suggest that although generally respondents would not use or approve the use of deceptive means to win unbelievers to faith in Christ, one in every four respondents would use or approve the use of even deceptive means in bringing non-believers to faith in Christ.

A large majority strongly agreed (80%) or agreed (10%) with the view that where there is spiritual maturity all Christians will be using their talents and spiritual gifts effectively, but some strongly disagreed (5%) or disagreed (1.3%) with this view or were neutral (2.6%) about it. It is noteworthy that, generally, effective use of talents and spiritual gifts by church members is positively associated with spiritual maturity.

More than a half of the respondents (51%) strongly disagreed and nearly one in eight (12%) disagreed with the view that in a church where there is spiritual maturity there is no need for church leaders because everyone is already empowered to make the correct decisions. But three in ten (31%) respondents strongly agreed (17%) or agreed (14%) with this view, and one in twenty (5%) were neutral about it.

The vast majority (81%) of the respondents strongly agreed with the view that a spiritually mature church has stability in sound knowledge and doctrine about Christ and all other teachings of their faith, and 10.3% agreed with the view. But some strongly disagreed (3.8%), disagreed (1.3%), or were neutral (2.6%). Also, 81% strongly agreed and nearly 12% others agreed with the view that where there is spiritual maturity the church has the ability to resist wrong influence, such as wrong teaching and wrong conduct. There were no respondents who strongly disagreed with this view, though a few disagreed (5.1%) with it or were neutral (2.6%) about it.

The vast majority strongly agreed (86%) or agreed (7.7%) with the view that where there is spiritual maturity, the church has the ability and orientation to distinguish truth from falsehood about the Christian faith. Very few strongly disagreed (1.3%) or disagreed (2.6%), and very few were neutral (1.3%).

The vast majority of the respondents strongly agreed (73%) or agreed (17%) with the view that where there is spiritual maturity the church has the ability and readiness to follow the truth and reject wickedness at all cost. A few respondents (5%) disagreed but none disagreed strongly, and an equal percentage of the respondents were neutral about the view.

Nearly a half (49%) of the respondents strongly agreed and nearly 17% others agreed with the view that where there is spiritual maturity Christians will speak the truth always in love, regardless of the nature of the truth and the nature of the audience. In contrast, about 27% disagreed with the view, about half of them (12%) disagreeing strongly, while some (5%) were neutral about it.

The vast majority of the respondents strongly agreed (89%) or agreed (3.8%) with the view that submission to God-ordained, authentic church authority is a sign of spiritual maturity. A few respondents strongly disagreed (3.8%) or were neutral (3.8%) about the view.

5.3 Discussion

5.3.1 Understanding of the Meaning and Essence of Spiritual Maturity

One of the key findings of the survey was that for the most accurate description of spiritual maturity, 67% chose "individual Christians being able to stand alone for the faith," 14% chose "ability to identify doctrinal error," and 14% chose "all Christians together accepting the whole truth about Christ." Very few (2.6%) chose "ability to cast out demons" or "ability to fast and pray for many days." This implies that the church leadership understood spiritual maturity primarily as a personal and individual stability and constancy in the faith, but much less as individual's ability to identify error or as corporate understanding of the truth. The ability to exercise the spiritual discipline of fasting and praying and ministerial ability of casting out demons were not considered highly as key descriptions of spiritual maturity.

Another key finding was that the majority (74%) of the respondents agreed—nearly half of them (36%) strongly—that spiritual maturity means that all the members of the church understand all the fundamental teachings about Christ the same way, while 9% were neutral and nearly 14%

disagreed including, 10% who strongly disagreed. From this finding it can be deduced that the church leadership that participated in the study generally understood unity of knowledge about Christ to be an aspect of spiritual maturity. However, this finding also shows that although there is generally an understanding that spiritual maturity means all members understand the fundamental teachings about Christ the same way, there was a significant percentage of respondents (24%) who did not hold this view, among whom half strongly disagreed. This implies diversity of understanding of the meaning of spiritual maturity. It is not clear whether the point of their disagreement was the aspect of knowing the fundamental teachings about Christ, or the impossibility or even the necessity of *all* believers understanding and upholding the fundamental teachings about Christ the same way. It therefore seems that there is some considerable degree of disagreement in aspects of the meaning of spiritual maturity as all Christians knowing the fundamental teachings about Christ. This means that the promotion of spiritual maturity would not require persuading the leadership with regard to the importance, but only explaining the meaning and the ultimate goal of spiritual maturity.

It was also found that nearly eight in ten (78%) respondents strongly agreed (41%) or agreed (37%) that spiritual maturity means that all the members of the church *accept* all the fundamental teachings about Christ the same way, and nearly one in five (19%) disagreed, with nearly half of them (9%) strongly disagreeing with that view, while 3.8% were neutral. These results indicate some notable diversity in understanding whether or not the meaning of spiritual maturity includes all members accepting the fundamental teachings about Christ the same way. Although the large majority at least agreed with the view, the nearly 20% who disagreed constitute a significant proportion of a different position. It is possible that this proportion of respondents disagreed with inclusiveness that all members accept every one teaching about Christ in the same way.

Another key finding was that 47% of the respondents strongly agreed that accepting Christ as Lord and Savior would normally follow after one attains some spiritual maturity, with nearly a third as many (15%) others agreeing with that view. One-fifth (21%) strongly disagreed and 3.8% disagreed with the view that accepting Christ as Lord and Savior would normally follow after one attains some spiritual maturity. Some respondents, though very few (2.6%), were neutral about this view. That means 62% of the respondents at least agreed that accepting Christ as Lord and Savior would normally follow after one attains some spiritual maturity, and only one in four (24.8%) at least disagreed that accepting Christ as Lord and Savior comes after one attains some level of spiritual maturity.

These results are surprising. It is possible that there was a lack or incorrect understanding of spiritual maturity. But results of the survey on the meaning of spiritual maturity, as well as the means by which spiritual maturity is to be attained, suggest that there was correct understanding of spiritual maturity. Alternatively, it could be proposed that there was lack of or an or erroneous understanding of the meaning of accepting Christ as Lord and Savior, but such a proposition is also highly doubtful. How possibly can the leadership from the supposedly evangelical tradition of the Anglican Church lack understanding of the meaning of accepting Christ as Lord and Savior? Obviously, lack or incorrect understanding of the essence of accepting Christ by faith as Lord and Savior and spiritual maturity, or both, would have a negative implication on the understanding of the relationship of the two. It appears that one in six church leaders who participated in the study understood that spiritual maturity precedes conversion, in which case faith in Christ would be a step after attaining some spiritual maturity. This would imply that some respondents would assume themselves as well as others to be spiritually mature even if they have not professed faith in Christ.

It was also found that most respondents strongly agreed (63%) or agreed (23%) with the view that the focus on bringing about spiritual maturity has to be more on the corporate life of the church and less upon individual Christians. This is a high proportion (86%) of the respondents at least agreeing that spiritual maturity is to focus on the corporate sense of the church and not the individual members. Some respondents, however, strongly disagreed (7.7%) or disagreed (5%) with this view, and very few (1.3%) were neutral. This particular finding stands in contrast with the finding discussed above, where emphasis of the essence of spiritual maturity was reflected as personal and individual stability and constancy in the faith but much less as the individual's ability to identify error or as corporate understanding of the truth. These two findings would be reconciled only by interpreting the corporate focus here in terms of understanding that all members individually are to have the focus on spiritual maturity.

Another key finding was that for the vast majority (87%) of the respondents spiritual maturity means acquiring the knowledge of the basic concepts about God and his word. For 76% of them it also means doing God's will and his word, and for 44% of them spiritual maturity means the individual's ability and capability to practice, experience, and live according to the purpose of God. When these percentages are taken into consideration, it seems that spiritual maturity means first acquiring a particular level of knowledge of concepts about God and a particular level and quality of the knowledge of God's word, then a particular level of ability to do the will of God and to know and follow God's will, and then ability and capability of the individual Christian to live a particular life, namely, that of living according to the purpose of God, in that order.

On the one hand, this configuration of the percentages implies an emphasis on the meaning of spiritual maturity as possession of conceptual knowledge about God and his word, followed by practical implementation of that conceptual knowledge in everyday life. On the other hand, it is not clear why practicing, experiencing, and living according to the purpose of God did not feature prominently as an aspect of spiritual maturity. Possibly the respondents understood that for every person there is a specific purpose of God, or that every person can know and live according to the purpose of God but that even so it is not central to the essence of spiritual maturity. It could also be hypothesized that because the purpose of God for one's life is definite and fixed prior to the person's birth (cf. Jer 1:4, 5, Lk 1:11–18) and therefore it does not depend on a person's faith—since God would have a purpose for every human being but not every human being would come to faith in Christ—then God's purpose for a person's existence is to be considered outside the realm of spiritual maturity, its centrality to life notwithstanding. Furthermore, it is possible that the concept of a purpose of God for one's life was too abstract, and the idea of living according to the purpose of God too unfamiliar, to the respondents. These possibilities are not unlikely for the kind of respondents in the study, but they are simply possibilities. What can be concluded here is that according to the respondents the meaning of spiritual maturity at least includes the acquisition of knowledge of God and God's will, and implementation of that knowledge in every day life.

These results suggest that the respondents understood spiritual maturity in terms of *knowledge* (of the basic concepts about God), *orientation* (towards doing the will of God and following the word), and *capability* (to do the will of God and to follow the word of God), in that order. The knowledge acquisition that constitutes spiritual maturity is the knowledge of basic concepts about God and knowledge of the Bible. If, as it appears to be the case, the respondents' understanding of spiritual maturity is in the order of knowledge, orientation, then capability, then a number of issues arise. The respondents did not indicate the actual content of the concepts about God and they were not expected to indicate concepts about God. It is possible that the respondents presume the very existence of God, the existence of concepts about God, and the possibility of knowing (and also not knowing) those concepts. There are concepts related, for example, to God's nature as holy, eternal, and triune; his character, as loving, merciful, gracious, and just; and his attributes such as omnipresence, omniscience, immutability, and omnipotence.[9]

The respondents understood that there is the will of God in general for all creation and possibly that there is the will of God for individuals. This is in line with the general understanding in theological circles.[10] Obviously, it is possible to lack knowledge of the will of God. A possibility also exists of not following the word of God, due to ignorance of the Bible, failure to follow the word of God, or lack of the ability to do so. According to this finding, spiritual maturity pertains to knowing and habitually following the will and the word of God.

It was also found that the vast majority of the respondents (83%) said unity demonstrates love, three quarters (74%) also said unity manifests spiritual maturity, 56% said spiritual maturity and love are the result of knowing God, and 15% said spiritual maturity and love allow members to exercise the gifts of the Holy Spirit. Thus, in terms of the relationship between spiritual maturity and unity in the church, love may be presumed to be an important element of spiritual maturity. In view of this particular finding of the present study, spiritual maturity will bring about love, and love will in turn be demonstrated by unity. Understanding spiritual maturity and unity as being the results of knowing God could imply that not only *both* spiritual maturity and unity but also *together* they originate from the same source, and together they enable as well as create an environment in which church members could exercise the gifts of the Holy Spirit. These results also show that spiritual maturity and unity co-originate and are together needed for the church members to be able to effectively exercise their spiritual gifts.

From the discussion in the preceding paragraphs it can be concluded that for the respondents in the present study, spiritual maturity is in essence a personal and individual stability and constancy in the faith, but much less

---

9. See Thiessen, *Lectures*, 75–99; Grudem, *Systematic Theology*, 141–51.
10. See for example Thiessen, *Lectures*, Grudem, *Systematic Theology*.

an individual's ability to identify error or as corporate understanding of the truth. It means *knowledge* (of the basic concepts about God), *orientation* (towards doing the will of God and following the word), and *capability* (to do the will of God and to follow the word of God), in that order. With some degree of disagreement, spiritual maturity means generally that Christians know and accept the fundamental teachings about Christ. Spiritual maturity was understood as acquiring a particular level of knowledge of concepts about God and a particular level and quality of the knowledge of God's word, then a particular level of ability to do the will of God and to know and follow God's will, and then ability and capability of the individual Christian to live a particular life, namely, that of living according to the purpose of God, in that order. Spiritual maturity and unity co-originate and are together needed for the church members to be able to effectively exercise their spiritual gifts. There was erroneous understanding that some level of spiritual maturity precedes conversion.

5.3.2   Understanding of the Means to Spiritual Maturity

It was found that one in four (26%) strongly agreed and 27% others agreed that the primary means towards attaining spiritual maturity are baptism and confirmation. One-fifth (21%) of the respondents strongly disagreed and 17% others disagreed with this view, and one in ten (10%) respondents were neutral about it. These results show a split of views among the respondents, with more than half (53%) understanding baptism and confirmation to be the primary means towards spiritual maturity, and the remaining 47% not considering, even strongly disagreeing, that baptism and confirmation are the primary means of spiritual maturity.

A number of issues are noteworthy with regard to this finding. First, it implies a difference in understanding the meaning and role of baptism and confirmation as well as their relationship with spiritual maturity. Second, that the majority of the respondents would see baptism and confirmation to be the primary means of spiritual maturity is rather surprising. A number of key questions arise from these findings and invite some theoretical explorations. The very diversity of understanding may suggest a lack of common understanding of the significance, purpose, or meaning of baptism and confirmation. Furthermore, since the two sacraments are actually events, not processes, and spiritual maturity is a process, how would baptism and confirmation be the primary means of attaining spiritual maturity? On the other and, since the respondents are church leaders, it would be expected of them to know the meaning, significance, and role of baptism and confirmation in the life of a Christian. It is rather more likely, from the point of view of this finding, that the leaders do not understand the meaning of spiritual maturity and how baptism and confirmation relate to it. It is also possible that these leaders hold such a high view of baptism and confirmation—and they would—that they consider them the most decisive variables in a Christian's spiritual journey. If this is the case, it betrays a ritualistic tendency on their part, and hence lack of spiritual maturity.

The key finding that nearly all respondents (99%) strongly agreed with is the view that in order for the church to grow towards spiritual maturity correct and systematic biblical teaching is necessary; and this is expected. However, there may be a need to explore what correct and systematic biblical teaching is and why it is necessary for the attainment of spiritual maturity. But this finding is consistent with the role of biblical instruction in achieving spiritual maturity in Ephesians 4:1–16. This means spiritual maturity is expected and that its implication for church ministers is to correctly and systematically teach the Bible.

It was also found that nearly 52.6% of the respondents strongly agreed with the view that, unlike salvation, spiritual maturity requires human effort to attain it, and about 7.7% agreed. However, more than one-fifth (22%) of the respondents strongly disagreed, 13% others disagreed with the view, and 3.8% were neutral. From these results, it appears that although six in ten (60.3%) understood the necessity of human effort in attaining spiritual maturity, more than a third of the respondents (35%) denied any necessity of human effort to contribute towards the attainment of spiritual maturity. Apparently, there is a lack of understanding of the need for human effort. As such, it is likely that there would be limited or no incentive, motivation, desire, or even receptivity to human contribution towards attaining spiritual maturity.

A further key finding was that the church leadership understood the means to attain spiritual maturity to be reading and understanding the Bible (87%), having a genuine relationship with Christ and trust in God (76%), having faith and performing acts of love (45%), and living a life of fasting and praying (31%). This finding means that the majority of the respondents here imply that spiritual maturity comes about through some human effort, *inter alia*, reading and understanding the Bible, performing acts of love, or fasting and praying. This variety of possible avenues that

The Mature Church

human efforts could employ in pursuit of spiritual maturity implies that acknowledging human responsibility in bringing about spiritual maturity may be one thing, and the accuracy and efficiency of the methods that could be used is another thing.

Thus, whether, for example, having faith and performing acts of love would contribute towards spiritual maturity would be debatable. It would be admissible that studying the Bible would contribute towards spiritual maturity, provided that the correct methods of studying the Bible are faithfully employed.[11] It would also be granted that a life of prayer and fasting would contribute towards spiritual maturity, if such fasting and praying are based on a sound biblical understanding.[12] Although the need for human effort in attaining spiritual maturity is apparently presumed, it is interesting to note that three in four of the respondents also implied that having a genuine relationship with Christ and trust in God would bring about spiritual maturity.

It is possible that there is a contradiction here: on the one hand acknowledging the necessity of the human factor in attaining spiritual growth, and on the other presuming spiritual maturity to be a natural or automatic outcome of having a genuine relationship with Jesus Christ and trusting God, without requiring any human contribution. However, it is more likely that the results here imply that the efficacy of human efforts in contributing towards spiritual maturity is only possible in the context of genuine faith in Christ and trust in God. This would be in line with the fact that without spiritual conversation[13] and the subsequent regeneration[14] a

---

11. The Bible and its message are valid and relevant to all peoples of all space and time. However, because the text of the Bible was written in specific temporal, social-cultural, and historical setting interpretation is necessary, and accurate interpretation requires not only discipline and due diligence but also the appropriate tools and methods correctly employed, premised on an understanding of the necessity of biblical interpretation (see Fee & Stewart, *How to Read*, 17–31; Virkler, *Hermeneutics*, 19–20; Corley, Student's Primer," 13–18; Klein, Blomberg, Hubbard, *Introduction* (2004), 3–4).

12. I would argue that whereas fasting and praying are meant to be expressions of the individual's resolve to discipline the body and mind in order to give the spiritual dimension the needed yielding, fasting and praying may be done, erroneously, as if to persuade God to do things, or to impress God or call upon his attention to the rescue of the person praying. Prayer and fasting, done in accordance with correct biblical knowledge, would contribute towards a life of deep devotion and sense of insight in the spiritual things, hence spiritual maturity.

13. See Grudem, *Systematic Theology*, 709–17; also Wilson, "Back to Conversation," 53–59.

14. See Grudem, *Systematic Theology*, 699–706.

person cannot possibly grow to spiritual maturity. The implication here is that the respondents would require as well as expect some human investment for the spiritual growth of Christians.

5.3.3 Understanding of the Indicators of Spiritual Maturity

One of the findings was that most leaders (87%) mentioned that the important indicators of spiritual maturity in the church include transformed members' lives whereby the members also demonstrate accurate understanding of the Bible, or faithful attendance and participation in church activities such as prayers, evangelism and outreach Programs (65%),, or increased church membership (64%). Some (39%) also mentioned financial giving for the work of God as an important indicator of spiritual maturity. These results suggest that spiritual maturity was understood in terms of observable behaviors of church members, primarily a reflection of correct knowledge of the Bible, but also active participation in church activities that would bring about further growth, hence spiritual reproduction, and contributing towards the sustenance or continuity of the work and life of the church. This finding is consonant with the expected understanding of spiritual maturity.

Another key finding was that a large majority of the respondents strongly agreed (80%) or agreed (10%) with the view that where there is spiritual maturity all Christians will be using their talents and gifts effectively. However, some strongly disagreed (5%) or disagreed (1.3%) with this view or were neutral (2.6%) about it. It is noteworthy that, generally, effective use of talents and spiritual gifts[15] by church members is positively associated with spiritual maturity. This finding is expected. The use of talents and spiritual gifts presumably requires awareness of the existence and possession of those gifts as well as the obedience to faithfully exercise those talents and spiritual gifts to the benefit of others. It is noteworthy here that the presence of talents and spiritual gifts in a person's life does not necessarily mean an automatic exercise of those talents and spiritual gifts.

---

15. I make a distinction between skills, talents, and spiritual gifts in order to respectively refer to exceptional abilities acquired through training and personal effort, exceptional abilities with which one is born, and exceptional abilities that become manifest in a person's life as a result of the bestowal by the Holy Spirit. With that distinction, anyone can have skills, and people are born with a variety of talents, but only a Christian can have spiritual gifts.

The finding here then is that it is spiritual maturity that makes possible the effective use of talents and gifts, which implies that the effective use of talents and spiritual gifts is an indicator of spiritual maturity. It was also found that nearly 80% of the respondents strongly agreed and 10% others agreed with the view that a spiritually mature church has stability in sound knowledge and doctrine about Christ and all other teachings of their faith. Possession of sound knowledge and doctrine about Christ is an important and valid indicator of spiritual maturity.

It was also found that about 81% of the respondents strongly agreed and about 12% others agreed with the view that where there is spiritual maturity the church has the ability to resist wrong influence. There were no respondents who strongly disagreed with this view, though a few disagreed (5%) or were neutral (2.6%). This finding is consistent with the finding in the preceding paragraph. Since spiritual maturity implies possession of sound knowledge and doctrine about Christ, it would be expected that spiritual maturity would contribute to a desire and ability to resist wrong influence. The impact of wrong influence would typically manifest itself in terms of doctrinal error, heresy, values, beliefs, practices, and behaviors that are inconsistent or are contrary to authentic biblical teaching.

This is in harmony with another finding whereby the vast majority of the respondents strongly agreed (86%) and 8% others agreed with the view that where there is spiritual maturity the church has the ability and orientation to distinguish truth from falsehood about the Christian faith. Very few strongly disagreed (1.3%), disagreed (2.6%), or were neutral (1.3%). Since spiritual maturity was associated with knowledge of the concepts of God, knowing and doing the will of God, and all Christians agreeing and accepting the basic teachings about Christ, it would be expected that spiritually mature Christians would also be characterized by an ability and orientation to distinguish truth from falsehood. Similarly, as another key finding showed, where there is spiritual maturity the church has the ability and readiness to follow the truth and reject wickedness at all costs. This finding is expected as an indicator of spiritual maturity. There is a reflection of expected unwavering commitment to the truth, truth here referring to Christian or biblical truth.

Interesting, however, is the finding that only about two-thirds (66%) of the respondents at least agreed (with 49% agreeing strongly) with the view that where there is spiritual maturity Christians will speak the truth always in love regardless of the nature of the truth and the nature of the

Spiritual Maturity in the Church: A Case Study

audience. As many as 27% disagreed with the view, with nearly half of them (12%) disagreeing strongly, and some (5%) were neutral. This implies some caution that even spiritually mature Christians may not necessarily speak the truth in love, regardless of the nature of the truth. It may be that the respondents acknowledge or hold a view that there will be times and circumstances whereby speaking the truth or speaking the truth in love may not be possible.

It was also found that nearly three quarters (73%) of the respondents strongly disagreed with the view that where the church is spiritually mature its members will tolerate doctrinal error and take no action about it, and 6.4% others disagreed. It would be expected that spiritual maturity would lead to responsible Christian living, whereby Christians would be the "salt of the earth" and "light of the world" (Matt 5:13–16). Surprisingly, nearly 12% of them agreed with the view that spiritual maturity would lead to tolerating doctrinal error, with some of them (2.6%) even agreeing strongly. Thus, generally, the respondents would not tolerate doctrinal error. It is not clear why spiritual maturity would be linked to the ability and tendency to tolerate doctrinal error. It is possible that those agreeing that if there is spiritual maturity Christians would tolerate doctrinal error may mean that either there would be no doctrinal error and so there would be nothing to tolerate, or that such doctrinal error would have no effect on spiritually mature Christians and so ignoring it would be all that will be needed.

5.3.4   Understanding of When or Whether Spiritual Maturity Will Be Complete

Another key finding was that six in ten (62%) respondents said spiritual maturity becomes complete when people change and accept Christ as their Lord and Savior, over half (53%) also said spiritual maturity becomes complete when church members correctly understand and keep the word of God, 36% of them said spiritual maturity becomes complete when there is correct teaching and understanding of the Bible, and one-third (33.3%) said spiritual maturity would become complete only when Christ returns. It is interesting to note that some (9%) said that spiritual maturity will never become complete in this life. The understanding that spiritual maturity will become complete when Christ returns in essence means the same thing as the understanding that spiritual maturity will never come to completion in this life. This finding shows that the church leaders in the study provided more than one marker of the completion of spiritual maturity. There was an apparent diversity of views and understanding with regard to the completion of spiritual maturity. The mention of accepting Christ as Lord and Savior as the point of completion of spiritual maturity, which was mentioned by the majority, is surprising. It may imply that the process to spiritual maturity would be taking place prior to acknowledging Christ as Lord and Savior, of which the latter would then be a culmination of that process. Or, it would imply that spiritual maturity is synonymous to acknowledging Christ as Lord and Savior, which of course is not correct. Since spiritual maturity is a process that would follow after conversion, both of these possible implications do not make sense to say the least, and may be erroneous.

The understanding that spiritual maturity becomes complete when church members correctly understand, teach, and keep the word of God reflects the ultimate state. If that be the case, then it would mean the church leadership understands that there is such a state that can be reached. Also, this understanding would be consistent with the understanding that either spiritual maturity would not become complete in this life or that it would at Christ's return. This implication of this understanding could be negative or positive. Negatively, the understanding that spiritual maturity would become complete at Christ's return or would never become complete could lead to the members' resignation from pursuing spiritual maturity. Positively, understanding that spiritual maturity would be realized at Christ's return could lead to continued pursuit of spiritual maturity. This is more likely to be the case, given the respondents' understanding that spiritual maturity would become complete when Christians correctly understand and follow the word of God.

5.3.5 Understanding of the Necessity of Spiritual Maturity

It was also found that the vast majority (89%) of the leaders said spiritual maturity is important for serving God fully, two-thirds (64%) said spiritual maturity is important for building up the church, seven in ten (69%) said spiritual maturity is important for understanding the Bible, one third (32%) said spiritual maturity is important for overcoming temptations, and nearly one-fourth (23%) said spiritual maturity is important for experiencing the manifestations of God's deeds, such as miracles. Thus, generally, church leadership in this study acknowledges the importance of spiritual maturity, as it provides the ability to serve God and to build the church, strength to overcome temptations, and the ability to experience divine manifestations. This is consonant with another finding: that 90% of the respondents strongly agreed that spiritual maturity is not just good but is necessary for the church, and 5% others agreed. Thus, largely, spiritual maturity was understood as necessary for the church. With this understanding of the importance of spiritual maturity, the latter should be the pursuit of every church member.

Another key finding was also that more than two-thirds of the respondents did not agree with the view that spiritual maturity is a good thing but is not all that necessary to grow to spiritual maturity. This is consistent with another finding in which the majority of the respondents strongly disagreed (63%) or disagreed (15%) with the view that spiritual maturity is a good thing but not all that necessary; but one in five strongly agreed (10%) or agreed (10%) with the view. Surprisingly, one in five strongly agreed (10.3%) or agreed (10.3%) that spiritual maturity is a good thing but is not all that necessary to grow to spiritual maturity, and 1.3% were neutral. Taking it conversely, these findings show that generally spiritual maturity was understood as necessary, not just good; but also a noticeable proportion of respondents (20.6%) had the view that it was not necessary. This is in line with the essence of Ephesians 4:1–16.

5.3.6 Level of Spiritual Maturity of the Church Leadership

It was found that the vast majority (89%) of the church leaders in the study thought that people who teach wrong doctrines in the church should be told in love that they are wrong. It is interesting to note that some (2.6%) said that such people should be allowed to continue or should be excommunicated, and half as many (1.3%) said such people should be punished severely. This implies that the leadership would rather confront the wrong teachers than keep quiet, and correct the wrong teachers lovingly rather than punish them severely. Similarly, nearly nine in ten respondents (87%) would respond to erroneous teaching by a church leader by explaining to the leader the truth in love, eight in ten (80%) would respond to such a situation by stopping the person, seven in ten (68%) would respond by praying for and warning the person, very few (3.8%) would rather desert the church leader teaching erroneous doctrines and follow others, and even fewer (2.6%) would simply keep quiet and do nothing lest they trigger a conflict.

It appears generally that the respondents would take some action in the event that a church leader gives erroneous teachings. These actions would include explaining to the leader that he or she is wrong, stopping the leader from teaching by some means, praying for and warning the leader of the consequences that could follow from the erroneous teachings, or by deserting the particular leader to follow other leaders in other churches. There is an apparent pattern here that decreasing numbers of respondents chose types of response as these types got increasingly passive. What this means is that the more active the course of action was, the more likely the leaders would choose it. Ideally, this is what would be expected; the response would be to approach the erring leader and in love confront the teaching with the intention to keep the erring leader, remain together, and correct the erroneous teaching (see Gal 6:2). In the event of unsuccessful attempts, more confrontational steps, such as barring or denying the person a platform from which to teach, would be resorted to. It is more likely that a church would have a system of dealing with such situations. Praying and giving appropriate warnings would be an alternative or an additional step to take in dealing with the situation. The results show here that some leaders would rather adopt a pessimist approach by deserting the erring leader.

Another key finding was that two-thirds (67%) of the respondents at least agreed, with most of them (54%) agreeing strongly, that when there is full spiritual maturity Christians will fiercely oppose other church members and church leaders who teach erroneous doctrines. About 14% strongly disagreed with this view, 13% others disagreed, and 6.4% were neutral. These results show some diversity of views. It is possible that respondents perceive it as a Christian duty to oppose erroneous teaching, even fiercely or vehemently. This would be, first an understanding of the possibility of erroneous teaching and secondly the understanding that it will always be necessary to oppose the erroneous teaching fiercely. On the other hand, those disagreeing to the suggested action against erroneous teaching may simply believe that there can be no such teachings and therefore there is nothing to oppose, let alone oppose fiercely. Therefore it will never be necessary to engage in any fierce opposition of erroneous teaching. But it is also possible that they may be dissenting to the fierce aspect of the opposing response to erroneous teaching. This diversity centres on two basic questions, namely, whether or not to respond to erroneous teaching, and in what way to respond to erroneous teachings.

Another key finding was that the majority of the respondents strongly disagreed (54%) or disagreed (15%) with the view that it is acceptable for the church to win unbelievers by any means, including deceiving and luring them so that by any means they get into the kingdom of God. Surprisingly, one in four (26%) respondents strongly agreed (14%) or agreed (12%) with the view, and 3.8% were neutral. These results suggest that although generally respondents would not use or approve the use of deceptive means to win unbelievers to faith in Christ, a significant percentage shows the contrary, whereby one in every four respondents would use or approve the use of any means, including deceptive ones, in bringing non-believers to faith in Christ. Therefore, whereas this is the view that would be expected, it is noteworthy that 26% of the respondents agreed, including 14% of them who agreed strongly that deception and any trickery could be used for evangelistic outreach purposes. It is possible that the church leaders in the study were so passionate about non-Christians that they would approve of the use of any means to win these non-Christians to faith in Christ.

5.4 Understanding and Level of Spiritual Maturity of the Church Leaders

5.4.1 The Meaning and Essence of Spiritual Maturity

Spiritual maturity has to be focused more on the corporate life of the church and less on individual Christians. As this finding was contrary to the finding that emphasized the essence of spiritual maturity as personal and individual stability and constancy in the faith, these two findings would be reconciled only by interpreting the corporate focus here in terms of understanding that all members individually are to be the focus on spiritual maturity. Spiritual maturity is in essence a personal and individual stability and constancy in the faith, but much less an individual's ability to identify error or as corporate understanding of the truth. It means *knowledge* (of the basic concepts about God), *orientation* (towards doing the will of God and following the word), and *capability* (to do the will of God and to follow the word of God), in that order.

With some degree of disagreement, spiritual maturity means generally that all Christians know and accept the fundamental teachings about Christ. Spiritual maturity was understood as acquiring a particular level of knowledge of concepts about God and a particular level and quality of the knowledge of God's word, then a particular level of ability to do the will of God and to know and follow God's will, and then an ability and capability of the individual Christian to live a particular life, namely, that of living according to the purpose of God, in that order. Spiritual maturity and unity co-originate and are together needed for the church members to be able to effectively exercise their spiritual gifts. There was the erroneous understanding that some level of spiritual maturity precedes conversion.

5.4.2 The Means to Spiritual Maturity

There was almost a polarization with regard to baptism and confirmation being the primary means towards spiritual maturity, suggesting a lack of common understanding of the significance, purpose, or meaning of baptism and confirmation, as well as the meaning of spiritual maturity and how baptism and confirmation relate to it. In order for the church to grow towards spiritual maturity, correct and systematic biblical teaching is necessary. This finding is consistent with the role of biblical instruction in achieving spiritual maturity according to Ephesians 4:1–16, that unlike salvation, spiritual maturity requires human effort to attain it. Hence the church leadership acknowledged the necessity of human effort in attaining spiritual maturity, although a substantial percentage denied any such necessity. Apparently, there is a lack of understanding of the need for human effort. As such, it is likely that there would be limited or no incentive, motivation, desire, or even receptivity to human contribution towards attaining spiritual maturity. Spiritual maturity comes about by some human effort. For the respondents, these are: reading and understanding the Bible, having a genuine relationship with Christ and trust in God, having faith and performing acts of love, and living a life of fasting and praying.

5.4.3 The Indicators of Spiritual Maturity

The important indicators of spiritual maturity are observable behaviors of church members, primarily a reflection of correct knowledge of the Bible, but also active participation in church activities that would bring about further growth, hence spiritual reproduction, and contributing towards the sustenance or continuity of the work and life of the church. Another indicator of spiritual maturity is that all Christians will be using their talents and gifts effectively, implying that it is spiritual maturity that makes possible the effective use of the talents and gifts. Other indicators are possession of and stability in sound knowledge and doctrine about Christ and all other teachings of faith, and the church's ability and orientation to resist wrong influence, such as through doctrinal error, heresy, values, beliefs, practices and behaviors that are inconsistent or are contrary to authentic biblical teaching. This means that the church has the ability and readiness to follow the truth and reject wickedness at all costs, implying a presumed unwavering commitment to biblical truth. Two more indicators are speaking the truth always in love regardless of the nature of the truth and the nature of the audience, and not tolerating doctrinal error and instead taking action about it.

5.4.4 When or Whether Spiritual Maturity Will Be Complete

Spiritual maturity becomes complete when people change and accept Christ as their Lord and Savior, when church members correctly understand and keep the word of God, when there is correct teaching and understanding of the Bible, and when Christ returns. If this does not happen, spiritual maturity will never become complete in this life.

5.4.5 The Necessity of Spiritual Maturity

The church leadership in this study acknowledged the importance of spiritual maturity, as it provides the ability to serve God and to build the church, understanding and doing the will of God, strength to overcome temptations, and ability to experience divine manifestations such as miracles, in that order. Generally, spiritual maturity was understood to be necessary for the church, not just good, but there was also a noticeable proportion of leaders who did not consider spiritual maturity as a necessity.

5.4.6 The Level of Spiritual Maturity of the Leadership

The general view was that when there is full spiritual maturity Christians will persistently oppose other church members and church leaders who teach erroneous doctrines, which may suggest a violent approach in dealing with doctrinal error. Leaders would rather confront the wrong teachers than keep quiet, and correct the wrong teachers lovingly rather than punish them severely. All of this suggests some good level of spiritual maturity. The courses of action they would take in response to erroneous teaching by a church leader are not only appropriate but also in agreement with what would be expected of spiritually mature people and a spiritually mature church—explaining to the leader the truth in love, or stopping the person, or praying for and warning the person. The general non-approval of winning non-Christians to the kingdom of God by use of any means, including deceiving and luring them, is expected for spiritually mature Christians. However, the significant percentage of the leaders approving the use of deceptive means to win non-Christians to faith in Christ is to be noted.

5.5 Summary

A survey was done among the leadership of the church in a specific context, to determine their understanding as well as their own level of spiritual maturity. This chapter provided explanation of the survey process, the data analysis and the findings, and a discussion of the key findings from which the meaning and essence of spiritual maturity and the level of spiritual maturity of the leadership were deduced. There are apparent dimensions of spiritual maturity, namely, the essence or meaning of spiritual maturity, the means of attaining maturity, indicators of spiritual maturity, time frame for completion of spiritual maturity, and the importance of spiritual maturity. Some of the dimensions are reflected more strongly and more clearly than others. The respondents also reflected a particular general level of spiritual maturity. In the next chapter, these dimensions are compared with and evaluated on the basis of the dimensions of spiritual maturity according to Ephesians 4:1–16, and the implications of the results are discussed.

6

Spiritual Maturity in Ephesians 4:13–16 and the Church:

Lessons from the Case Study

6.1 Introduction

ONE OF THE OBJECTIVES of this study is to compare spiritual maturity in Ephesians 4:13–16 with the understanding and level of spiritual maturity of the leadership of the church, and to draw implications for the work of the church. The meaning of spiritual maturity and its various dimensions has been established in chapter 4. The understanding of spiritual maturity and level of spiritual maturity of the leadership of the church has been established in chapter 5. The purpose of this chapter is to compare the meaning of spiritual maturity in Ephesians 4:13–16 with the understanding of spiritual maturity of the leadership of the church. The comparison is done along the dimensions of spiritual maturity, after which key implications of the results of the comparison for the work of the church are identified and discussed.

6.2 Comparing Spiritual Maturity in Ephesians 4:13–16 and the Understanding of Spiritual Maturity of Church Leadership

Dimension of spiritual maturity	Spiritual maturity according to Ephesians 4:13–16	Spiritual maturity according to church leadership
Meaning and essence	Spiritual maturity is a specific final and discernible destination. Arrival at this destination is supposed to be for all Christians, who increasingly become "one" as they approach the destination.	Spiritual maturity means possession of a particular level and quality of knowledge (of the basic concepts about God and God's will), attainment of a particular level of orientation (towards doing the will of God and following the word), and individual Christians possessing a particular level of capability to live a particular life (to do the will of God and to follow the word of God).
		Spiritual maturity has to be more on the corporate life of the church and less upon individual Christians.
	Spiritual maturity is in essence corporate in that it intends that all Christians grow together, towards that final state, progressively becoming one body.	Spiritual maturity is a personal and individual stability and constancy in the faith, but much less as individual's ability to identify error or as corporate understanding of the truth.
		With some degree of disagreement, spiritual maturity means generally that all Christians know and accept the fundamental teachings about Christ.
		Some level of spiritual maturity precedes conversion.

Dimension of spiritual maturity	Spiritual maturity according to Ephesians 4:13–16	Spiritual maturity according to church leadership
Means of attainment	Spiritual maturity is a sequel of the ministry participation of all Christians as started off and continuously equipped and guided by the ministers Christ appointed and gave as gifts.	To some leaders, baptism and confirmation are the primary means towards spiritual maturity.
	Biblical instruction is necessary for spiritual maturity to occur.	For spiritual maturity to occur, correct and systematic biblical teaching is necessary.
	All are to strive towards spiritual maturity.	Attainment of spiritual maturity requires human effort, although a substantial percentage denied any such necessity.
	Spiritual maturity is a product of salvation, and it requires sustained human effort, to attain or to be moving towards the goal.	Spiritual maturity comes about by some human effort, namely, reading and understanding the Bible, having a genuine relationship with Christ and trust in God, having faith and performing acts of love, and living a life of fasting and praying.
Point of attainment of spiritual maturity	In theory, the point for attaining spiritual maturity is anytime when the whole church will have attained the goal, when the church has grown to become an appropriate body, befitting as well as worthy of the Head, Christ.	Spiritual maturity becomes complete when people accept Christ as their Lord and Saviour.
		Spiritual maturity becomes complete when church members correctly understand and keep the word of God.
	Practically, the duration of attaining the goal of ultimate spiritual maturity is at consummation, when Christ returns, because each time there is a new convert to the Christian faith and who will need to be made a disciple, the configuration changes back to a state of overall spiritual immaturity.	Spiritual maturity becomes complete when there is correct teaching and understanding of the Bible.
		Spiritual maturity becomes complete when Christ returns; thus: spiritual maturity will never become complete in this life.

The Mature Church

Dimension of spiritual maturity	Spiritual maturity according to Ephesians 4:13–16	Spiritual maturity according to church leadership
Indicators of progression towards spiritual maturity		Observable behaviours of church members, primarily a reflection of correct knowledge of the Bible.
	Stability and constancy in the truth.	
	Ability to discern error and reject or correct it.	
	Ability and predisposition to speak the truth in love.	
	Meaningful participation of all members through effective use of their spiritual gifts, to the good of the whole church.	Active participation in church activities that would bring about further growth, hence spiritual reproduction.
	Unity of all, occurring by default when there is spiritual maturity. Hence, maturity will bring about unity, but not the other way round.	
		Contributing towards the sustenance or continuity of the work and life of the church.

Spiritual Maturity in Ephesians 4:13–16 and the Church

Dimension of spiritual maturity	Spiritual maturity according to Ephesians 4:13–16	Spiritual maturity according to church leadership
Specific key indicators of spiritual maturity	Speaking the truth in love.	Speaking the truth always in love regardless of the nature of the truth and the nature of the audience.
		Not tolerating doctrinal error and instead taking action about it.
	Meaningful and continued participation of the individual members in the building up of the body of Christ.	All Christians using their talents and spiritual gifts effectively, since it is spiritual maturity that makes possible the effective use of the talents and spiritual gifts.
		Possession of and stability in sound knowledge and doctrine about Christ and all other teachings of the Christian faith.
		Ability and orientation to resist wrong influence, such as doctrinal error, and values, beliefs, practices and behaviours that are inconsistent with or contrary to the Bible.
		Ability and readiness to follow the truth and reject wickedness at all cost, implying an unwavering commitment to biblical truth.

The Mature Church

Dimension of spiritual maturity	Spiritual maturity according to Ephesians 4:13–16	Spiritual maturity according to church leadership
Necessity of spiritual maturity: Lack of spiritual maturity is a dangerous state for the Christians	Spiritual maturity is necessary, because without it Christians will not stop being children (figuratively speaking).	Spiritual maturity is important for serving God fully.
	There is a call for the church to grow towards full spiritual maturity.	Spiritual maturity is important for building up the church.
	Without spiritual maturity, the church risks being in great danger.	Spiritual maturity is important for understanding the Bible.
	Spiritual immaturity implies a lack of intelligence and is characterized by instability and susceptibility to deception and to being led astray; being unstable, lacking in direction, and being open to manipulation.	Spiritual maturity is important for overcoming temptations.
	Lack of spiritual maturity will lead to Christians being volatile in their beliefs, unstable, foolish and incapable of understanding the truth.	Spiritual maturity is important for experiencing the manifestations of God's deeds such as miracles.
	An immature church will be in a state of confusion and lack of direction, instead of being goal-oriented.	
	Immature Christians are prone to succumb to false instruction, with adverse repercussions for faith living.	
	Spiritual immaturity lays Christians open to manipulation by cunning people and forces of error, and makes them easy prey to false teachings.	Spiritual maturity is needed to facilitate Christians to effectively exercise their spiritual gifts.
	Lack of spiritual maturity will mean Christians individually remain unable to discern and reject or oppose false teachings.	
	Since spiritual maturity brings with it the capacity to emulate various forms of teaching—accepting what is true and rejecting what is not, lack of spiritual maturity would be a grave matter for the church.	

Spiritual Maturity in Ephesians 4:13–16 and the Church

Dimension of spiritual maturity	Spiritual maturity according to Ephesians 4:13–16	Spiritual maturity according to church leadership
Necessity of spiritual maturity: false teachers, false teachings and their methods are difficult to discern and resist	Christians can expect to face false teachings	Spiritual maturity provides the ability to serve God and to build the church.
		Spiritual maturity provides the ability to understand and do the will of God.
		Spiritual maturity provides strength to overcome temptations.
	Immature Christians would fall easy prey to every new theological trend.	Spiritual maturity provides the ability to experience divine manifestations such as miracles.
	The false teachers are intentional and ready to do everything possible to deceive, mislead, and destroy	Generally, spiritual maturity is necessary for the church, not just good, but to many leaders it is not necessary.

6.3 Evaluation of the Church Leaders' Understanding of Spiritual Maturity

6.3.1 Meaning and Essence of Spiritual Maturity

There is some degree of agreement on the meaning and essence of spiritual maturity as understood by the leadership of the church and what Ephesians 4:13 presents. The areas of concurrence in this regard are the attainment of a particular state for all individual Christians defined by particular levels of knowledge and acceptance of that knowledge. However, there are some significant differences, even in the general areas of concurrence.

First, there are apparent differences on some aspects of the corporate essence of spiritual maturity. Whereas the text emphasizes a final destination or state entailing all Christians becoming one, the church leadership conceives the "corporate" sense of spiritual maturity in terms of including all individual Christians in programs aimed to achieve spiritual maturity. The position of the leaders that spiritual maturity has to be more on the corporate life of the church and less upon individual Christians is countered by the view that spiritual maturity is a personal and individual stability and constancy in the faith. The implications of understanding the corporate essence of spiritual maturity this way are apparent. Of course there would be inadequate focus on programming for spiritual maturity, as these programs will not likely pursue a final state of the whole church. Whereas the corporate essence in Ephesians 4:13 projects an expectation of increasing oneness of the body as the body progresses towards maturity, the understanding of the leaders of the corporate essence of spiritual maturity would lead to a focus on developing the abilities and constancy of all individual Christians to be able to stand on their own. The church leaders' understanding of the corporate essence of spiritual maturity simply misses the correct corporate essence of spiritual maturity according to the text. Thus, whether or not there will be some negative consequences is immaterial.

Second, the possession of a particular level and quality of knowledge (of the basic concepts about God and God's will), attainment of a particular level of orientation (towards doing the will of God and following the word), and individual Christians possessing a particular level of capability to live a particular life (to do the will of God and to follow the word of God) would correspond with the implied qualities expected of Christians who "are no longer children." What this means is that it should not be difficult for the church leadership to discuss and develop spiritual growth programs for the members. However, there are also differences with regard to knowledge. Whereas in the text the object of knowledge is the Son of God, Jesus Christ, the subject of the knowledge is God, God's word, and God's will.

The disagreement among the leaders themselves with regard to the fact that spiritual maturity means that all Christians know and accept the fundamental teachings about Christ confirms their understanding that neither is Christ the object of the knowledge nor is possessing "the knowledge of Christ" a key aspect of spiritual maturity. The text also suggests, as a key element of spiritual maturity, the ability to discern or recognize doctrinal error, especially about Christ, and to stand firm against it, but the church leaders considered spiritual maturity as much less individual Christians' ability to identify error as corporate understanding of the truth. There was even a serious error in the understanding of some of the church leaders that some level of spiritual maturity precedes confession of Christ as Lord and Savior. The implications here also are significant.

6.3.2 The Means to Attainment of Spiritual Maturity

From Ephesians 4:11–16, spiritual maturity is a sequel of the ministry participation of all Christians as started off and continuously equipped and guided by the ministers Christ appointed and gave to the church as gifts. In contradistinction, some church leaders in this study understood baptism and confirmation to be the primary means towards spiritual maturity. Being almost equally divided in understanding whether or not baptism and confirmation are the primary means of attaining spiritual maturity reflects a lack of common understanding of the significance, purpose, and meaning of baptism and confirmation as well as the relationship between spiritual maturity and these two church rites. Thus, at least in this respect, there was a major difference between the primary means of attaining spiritual maturity according to Ephesians 4:13–16 on the one hand, and the understanding of the means of attaining spiritual maturity among the leaders of the church, on the other. The implications here could be grave. With this understanding, the church leaders would consider generally that all baptized and confirmed members have attained spiritual maturity. Since most members are baptized at infancy and are confirmed at about the age of twelve years, the leaders would consider them spiritually mature. But this is simply inconceivable, at least from the standpoint of Ephesians 4:13, where it is clear that striving for spiritual maturity will likely continue till

The Mature Church

Christ's return. What this means then is that with this understanding of the means of spiritual maturity the leadership would be handicapped in terms of putting in place programs that would truly lead to spiritual maturity.

Ephesians 4:13 implies that all Christians are to strive towards spiritual maturity. The understanding of the church leaders in the study was that attainment of spiritual maturity requires human effort, although a substantial percentage denied any such necessity. Also, from Ephesians 4:13 it is clear that biblical instruction is necessary for spiritual maturity to occur. In consonance with the position of Ephesians 4:13, the leaders' understanding was also that for spiritual maturity to occur correct and systematic biblical teaching is necessary. Thus, except for the percentage of leaders that denied the necessity of human effort, generally, the leaders' understanding of the necessity of human effort in attaining spiritual maturity was in agreement with the position implied by Ephesians 4:13.

There may be some differences in the degree of the necessity of human effort, whereby, on the one hand, Ephesians 4:11–16 calls for a certain level of dedication so that all Christians continuously strive to grow spiritually, and on the other, the leaders simply recognize that all Christians are individually and personally supposed to make some effort to contribute towards their spiritual growth. But any such difference would only be a difference of degree, not of kind, and should not therefore be taken as significant. If the necessity of human effort in the process of attaining spiritual maturity is not acknowledged, little or no such efforts will be made. That means there would be no investment in terms of time, resources, training, and planning in relation to pursuing spiritual maturity. However, the leaders' understanding was that spiritual maturity comes about by some human effort, namely, reading and understanding the Bible, having a genuine relationship with Christ and trust in God, having faith and performing acts of love, and living a life of fasting and praying. This is quite in agreement with the implication of the meaning of spiritual maturity according to Ephesians 4:11–13 that spiritual maturity is a product of salvation and it requires sustained human effort to attain or to be moving towards the goal.

6.3.3 The Point of Attainment of Spiritual Maturity

In theory, according to Ephesians 4:13 the point at which spiritual maturity is attained is when the whole church will have attained the goal, when the church has grown to become an appropriate body, befitting as well as worthy of the Head, Christ. However, practically, as each time there is a new convert to the Christian that one will need to be discipled, the configuration changes back to a state of spiritual immaturity, and as new believers continue to join the church, the duration of attaining the goal of ultimate spiritual maturity is at consummation, when Christ returns. The leaders' understanding that spiritual maturity becomes complete when Christ returns, and thus that spiritual maturity will never become complete in this life, was in agreement with the position that full spiritual maturity would be at consummation, as Ephesians 4:13 implies.

The understanding of the church leaders that spiritual maturity becomes complete when people change and accept Christ as their Lord and Savior could be a drawback in making programs for their own spiritual growth as well as for the members. This is because with this understanding the leaders might view themselves and others as spiritually mature just because they have accepted Christ as Lord and Savior, when in fact that is only the starting point of the lifelong journey to spiritual maturity.

However, the leaders' understanding that spiritual maturity becomes complete when church members correctly understand and keep the word of God, or when there is correct teaching and understanding of the Bible, is of lower degree or essence compared to the point of completion implied by Ephesians 4:13, namely, when the church grows to attain a body befitting the Head, Christ. It seems to me that it is likely for individual Christians to attain a level of correct understanding of and ability to keep the word of God and for the church to not yet be a truly grown body that befits Christ as its Head.

6.3.4 The Indicators of Progression towards Spiritual Maturity

Whereas Ephesians 4:13–16 shows the indicators of progression towards spiritual maturity to be stability and constancy in the truth, ability of the church to discern error and reject or correct it, and ability and predisposition of the church to speak the truth in love, the indicators mentioned by the church leaders are somewhat different. The three indicators of progression towards spiritual maturity deduced from the Ephesians 4:13–16 seem to pertain to holding to the truth, the ability to identify and reject doctrinal error, and the ability and orientation to confront doctrinal error. Thus, the indicators in the text generally pertain to truth and error.

In contrast, indicators of progression towards spiritual maturity mentioned by the church leaders—meaningful participation of all members in the church through the effective use of their spiritual gifts, observable behaviors primarily reflecting correct knowledge of the Bible, active participation in church activities that would bring about further numerical growth, and contributing towards the sustenance or continuity of the work and life of the church—pertain to "normal" everyday life. This may reflect naiveté and even ignorance of the possibility of error and the possibility of departing from the truth. I argue that what the church leaders mentioned as the indicators of progression towards spiritual maturity are superficial reflections and are, strictly speaking, possible outcomes of spiritual maturity. Thus, whereas Ephesians 4:13–16 presents indicators of progression towards spiritual maturity to be growing in the ability to remain in the truth, to identify and reject error, and both to correct error and to do so in love, the church leaders mentioned indicators that would reflect general Christian living, not necessarily spiritual maturity.

All the indicators the church leaders mentioned can be presented in the life of a Christian or a Christian community, even if there is no spiritual maturity. For example, it is possible for a Christian to participate meaningfully in church activities and yet be spiritually immature, or one could reflect good observable behaviors, actively participate in church activities that would lead to growing membership, and contribute money for the work of the church even without being a Christian, let alone not being spiritually mature. But in agreement with the teaching in Ephesians 4:13–16, the church leaders understood that unity is a reality that occurs by default when there is spiritual maturity, meaning that maturity will bring about unity, but not the other way round.

6.3.5 Specific Key Indicators of Spiritual Maturity

One of the specific indicators of spiritual maturity according to the leaders of the church was speaking the truth always in love, regardless of the nature of the truth and the nature of the audience. Part of this understanding was their view that where there is spiritual maturity there will be no tolerance of doctrinal error and instead action will be taken about it. This specific indicator is similar to one of the key specific indicators of spiritual maturity stated in Ephesians 4:13–16, namely, speaking the truth in love.[1] Since the position in 4:13–16 is in the context that includes the manner of responding to error, it presumes the necessity to do so. If that be the case, then

---

1. See Eph 4:15.

the other indicators of spiritual maturity mentioned by the church leaders confirm this agreement. The other indicators mentioned are possession of and stability in sound knowledge and doctrine about Christ and all other teachings of the faith, the church having the ability and orientation to resist wrong influence, and the church having the ability and readiness to follow the truth and reject wickedness at all costs, implying a presumed unwavering commitment to biblical truth. The other specific indicator of spiritual maturity according to the church leaders, namely, all Christians using their talents and spiritual gifts effectively, was in consonance with the specific indicator of spiritual maturity according to Ephesians 4:13–16, namely, meaningful and continued participation of the individual members in the continuing building up of the body of Christ.

It appears, then, that the church leaders' understanding of the specific indicators of spiritual maturity was largely in agreement with the specific indicators of spiritual maturity according to Ephesians 4:1–16.

6.3.6 The Necessity of Spiritual Maturity

Generally, the church leaders understood spiritual maturity to be necessary for the church, not just good, but there was also a noticeable proportion of them who did not consider spiritual maturity as necessary. The part of the church leadership that understood that spiritual maturity is necessary for the church is in agreement with the apparent position presented in Ephesians 4:11–16, whereby spiritual maturity is presented as necessary, lest Christians do not stop being children, figuratively speaking. But the significant portion of the leaders that did not understand spiritual maturity to be necessary is to be noted. The implication of this is that generally it would not be necessary to persuade the leadership to make programs for their spiritual growth as well as that of the members they lead, but those leaders who did not understand spiritual maturity as necessary might not readily support any such programs.

According to the church leaders, the importance of spiritual maturity, or the reason why spiritual maturity is necessary, is that spiritual maturity provides the ability to serve God, for example, by facilitating Christians to effectively exercise their spiritual gifts and to build the church, to have strength to overcome temptations, and to have the ability to experience divine manifestations such as miracles. Except for the understanding that spiritual maturity brings about strength for Christians to overcome temptations, the rest of these aspects portray spiritual maturity as important or good, rather than necessary. This means that the weight the church leaders placed on spiritual maturity is less than the weight given to it in Ephesians 4:11–16.

In sharp contrast, Ephesians 4:13–16 calls for the church to grow towards full spiritual maturity, and in so doing shows that without spiritual maturity the church risks being in great danger, further showing that lack of spiritual maturity predisposes Christians to instability and susceptibility to deception and to being led astray, and openness to manipulation. Furthermore, as Ephesians 4:13–16 shows the consequences and conditions of lack of spiritual maturity, the gravity of the importance of the spiritual maturity is underlined. Lack of spiritual maturity will lead to Christians being volatile in their beliefs, unstable, foolish, and incapable of understanding the truth, and will make them remain prone to perversion of false instruction with adverse repercussions for faith living. As such, Christians will lay open to manipulation by cunning people and forces of error and continue to be easy prey to false teachings, with no ability to discern and reject or oppose dangerous false teachings.

Thus, whereas Ephesians 4:13–16 presents spiritual maturity to be of absolute necessity for the continued survival and propagation of the church, and lack of it as a grave matter for the church, the church leaders did not show an understanding of the weight of spiritual maturity anywhere close to that. These church leaders' understanding of the necessity of spiritual maturity reflects lack of awareness about, or an indifference to, the fact that Christians can expect to face false teachings, over against the unity of faith and knowledge of the Son of God, including the various religious philosophies and anti-Christian religions; and the fact that immature Christians would fall easy prey to every new theological propagation brought about by the false teachers—who are poised to do everything possible to deceive, mislead, and destroy.

6.4 Evaluation of the Level of Spiritual Maturity and Its Implications

One of the objectives of the study is to determine the level of spiritual maturity of the leadership of the church. The level of spiritual maturity will be reflected by the knowledge, expected behavior, and general orientation of the church leaders. The general understanding of the church leaders was that when there is full spiritual maturity Christians will fiercely oppose

Spiritual Maturity in Ephesians 4:13 and the Church

other church members and church leaders who teach erroneous doctrines. As this suggests or implies the possibility of resorting to a violent approach to dealing with doctrinal error, it reflects a low level of spiritual maturity.

That the church leaders would rather confront the wrong teachers than keep quiet, and rather correct the wrong teachers lovingly than punish them severely, suggests that the leaders would take action or support the taking of action against doctrinal error and would use or support the use of what would be acceptable approaches, namely corrective rather than punitive actions. Holding a view of the necessity to take action against doctrinal error, and an orientation to use constructive approaches to confronting error, suggests some good level of spiritual maturity on the part of the church leaders. Furthermore, the courses of action they would take in response to erroneous teaching by a church leader, namely, explaining to the leader the truth in love, stopping the person, or praying for and warning the person, are not only appropriate but also in agreement with what would be expected of spiritually mature people and a spiritually mature church.

The general non-approval of winning non-Christians to faith in Christ by use of any means, including deceiving and luring them so that by any means they get into the kingdom of God, is what would be expected of spiritually mature Christians. However, the significant percentage of the leaders who would approve the use of deceptive means to win non-Christians to faith in Christ is to be noted. This implies that, although generally there was a notable level of spiritual maturity, there was a major segment of the church leaders that reflected lack of spiritual maturity. I would argue that even if only some of the leaders display lack of spiritual maturity, it is not unreasonable to suspect that many of the members would also lack spiritual maturity. Inevitably, this condition would make not only the leaders but also the members vulnerable to deception, trickery, and false teachings, as well as fail to be fruitful members of the body of Christ, the church.

6.5 Summary

This chapter has evaluated the understanding of spiritual maturity of the leadership of the church in a specific context against the dimensions of spiritual maturity according to Ephesians 4:1–16. It has been found that the church's understanding of spiritual maturity concurs with only some of the dimensions of spiritual maturity found in the Scripture passage. There are several dimensions of spiritual maturity where the church is not in agreement with Ephesians 4:1–16, and sometimes it is even contrary to what the this Scripture passage teaches or implies with regard to spiritual maturity. The areas of disagreement pose significant implications for the work of the church. Also, the level of spiritual maturity of the church has been evaluated and it has been found that although there are several key indicators portraying the church as having some spiritual maturity, there are others that suggest an inadequate level of spiritual maturity and lack of common understanding of spiritual maturity. Again, a number of implications have been identified.

7

Conclusion

THE FOCUS OF THIS study is a rhetorical-critical interpretation of Ephesians 4:1–16 in order to determine the meaning of spiritual maturity and to demonstrate its use to evaluate the understanding and level of spiritual maturity of the church in a specific context. Following a survey and evaluation of selected methods of rhetorical criticism, a method of rhetorical criticism deemed appropriate for the interpretation of Ephesians 4:13 was developed and applied. The elements of the method were to determine the rhetorical context, determine the rhetorical dimensions of the first recipients, determine the rhetorical dimensions of the author, determine the rhetorical dimensions of the text, and then deduce authorial meaning and intended impact. From the interpretation process, the key dimensions of the meaning of spiritual maturity were obtained, namely, its meaning and essence, the means of attaining it, the point of attaining it, and the key indicators of progression towards it. From a baseline survey conducted among the leaders of a church in a particular setting, their understanding and level of spiritual maturity were determined and evaluated using the dimensions of spiritual maturity.

One important question that needs to be addressed is: What is the significance of Paul's Epistle to the Ephesians for the church and the world of modern times? Ephesians was written in the first century AD and in light of the realities of the first readers. One might be tempted to think that much of what the Apostle Paul is writing about in the epistle has little relevance for today. Nothing could be farther from the truth. The epistle is as much relevant, if not even more relevant, today as it was then. First, the basic truths of the first readers are valid for people of all time. God's plan of redemption predates and will outlive humanity. Therefore all peoples of all places and all times are covered by this everlasting stretch of the redemption plan, and therefore, also all those who will become believers; it shall

The Mature Church

be upon them to mature spiritually and live according to their calling. No one at any time who has believed Christ and become a new creation is exempted from living according to their new identity and fulfilling the responsibility and call of duty as witnesses of the love of God through Christ to all humanity. This is to be so regardless of the challenges and opposing forces that may and will arise from time to time as history continues to unfold. Thus the message of Ephesians is always alive and relevant.

But there is a second question, and perhaps a more pertinent one, that needs to be addressed: Just what is the relevance and importance of the subject spiritual maturity for the church in modern times, and what does it call for? Spiritual maturity remains of critical importance for the church. But often spiritual maturity is not understood or is misunderstood, and even when it is understood correctly little or nothing is done about it. Spiritual maturity is not the same as holding a position or playing a certain role in the church. It is also different from one's duration in the faith or one's possession of academic knowledge, including advanced theological or biblical knowledge. A number of areas of concern would underline the importance of the subject of spiritual maturity for modern times.

First, the identity of all Christians of all ages is the same, based on the divine grace revealed and accessible through Christ. By the same token, the general Christian responsibility to live in accordance with that identity is also the same for Christians throughout the ages. It would then follow that all Christians are called to spiritual maturity, to become the body befitting the Head, Christ, and the community that will fulfill its responsibility in the world.

Second, throughout the history of the church there have been numerous times when the church, as the body of Christ, has been confronted by opposing forces. The writings of the Apostle Paul indicate, on numerous occasions, that there will come times when not only false doctrines will be numerous but also those doctrines will receive credence.[1] These times seem to be with us as we experience another wave of these issues and challenges that are always poised to confront the church. The contents of the arguments opposed to the divine nature of Christ would inevitably constitute a pollution of the doctrinal environment within and around the church. Also, there are pervasive writings about Christ, such as Dan Brown's (2004) *The Da Vinci Code*,[2] in which generally good and historically acceptable

---

1. See 1 Tim 1:3–4; 4:1–5; 3:1–13; 6:3–5; 2 Tim 3:1–9; 4:2–4; Titus 1:10–11, 16.
2. *The Da Vinci Code* has of course been countered by authentic and accurate

Conclusion

information about Christ is subtly mixed with serious misinformation about Christ's life on earth and a general gross misrepresentation of Christ's social life.

Third, in the highly commercialized religious environment of our time, there seems to have arisen some preachers that one could refer to as preachers of another gospel and teachers of another Bible. In their teaching and preaching they seem to focus on the so-called gospel of prosperity, emphasizing that once (and if) one is a true follower of Christ it should follow that one's economic and social life, including one's health condition, will permanently change for the better. And this is supposed to hold true for every follower of Christ. It is claimed that all that is required for that change to take place is for one to exhibit positive confessions of success and prosperity, and to claim the promises of God in the Bible.[3] As such, these preachers and teachers deny any possibilities of pain and suffering due to such circumstances as poverty and sickness for Christians. Not only is such preaching and teaching untrue but it is in fact contrary to other parts of the Bible. The account of the extreme sufferings that Job[4] went through, the teaching of Christ himself that his followers would suffer,[5] Paul's thorn in the flesh,[6] the teachings through other New Testament writers,[7] the manner in which most of the disciples[8] and Christians in the first and second centuries died and, more recently, the Uganda martyrs,[9] all attest to the

---

information; see Garlow, *Da Vince Code Breaker*; Lutzer, *Da Vinci Deception*; and Kennedy, *Da Vinci Myth*.

3. There is a place of positive confession and living in accordance with the promises of God, but that positive confession and the promises of God do not preclude difficult times and trying circumstances. In Isa 43:2 for example, the promise is not that there will be no "rivers" and "fires," but that God will be with his people even in those times when they must go through such circumstances. According to the biblical account, for example, God did not put off the fire of Nebuchadnezzar's furnace nor change Nebuchadnezzar's decision, but he "came down" into the furnace and rescued Meshack, Shadrach, and Abednego (Dan 3); nor did God kill the lions in the den so that Daniel would be safe, but he folded the claws of the lions and made them not to harm Daniel (Dan 6:19–24).

4. Whereas one might argue that Job was not a Christian, we know it is the same God, the Father of our Lord Jesus Christ, who allowed the suffering that befell Job.

5. See Matt 10:28, 34–39; 24:21,22.

6. 2 Cor 12:7–10.

7. See for example Phil 1:29–30; 1 Pet 5:9–10.

8. For an excellent explanation of the lives of the twelve apostles of Christ, including how each one of them died, see MacArthur, *Twelve Ordinary Men*.

9. See Pirouet, *Black Evangelists*, 3.

fact that Christians are not exempt from pain and suffering and that they could suffer and die for their faith.[10] Furthermore, the Bible gives explicit warnings about the corrupting potential and tendency of wealth and riches, and calls for godliness and contentment.[11] Furthermore, Christ wants his followers to be able to trust God for all their needs.[12]

On the one hand, because of the strong appeal of their teaching and preaching and, possibly, a basic human desire to prosper and hedonistic inclinations, the preachers and teachers of another gospel attract huge crowds of followers, most of them Christians. These preachers and teachers are in the church, they mention and use the name Jesus, and they read from the Bible. Therefore their authority is taken for granted and what they preach and teach is also readily accepted. On the other hand, many a Christian does not have the ability to discriminate between what is authentic biblical teaching or scriptural and what is wrong and heretical, and does not assume their Christian responsibility "to speak the truth in love" against such teachings. In my view, besides the anti-Christian religions such as Islam,[13] and poor, bad, or lacking church leadership, these preachers of another gospel and teachers of another Bible constitute the most serious threat to the church. Some of these preachers and teachers purport to be operating through unusual anointing and emphasize an inclination towards divine manifestations such as people falling down as a sign of the powerful move of God in their lives and as a confirmation that the preacher or teacher is truly anointed of God. Christ is often presented—wrongly of course—as simply a miracle worker, satisfier of the emotional and even sexual needs of those who follow him, and a provider of money, food, and jobs. There is a distorted, unbiblical image of Christ, both in teaching about who he is and in presenting what he supposedly does. It is clear that spiritual maturity is a central part of the answer to these and similar trends.

Fourth, there are philosophies within the worldwide church confronting Christians. In my view, these philosophies are often based on heretical interpretation of the Bible, often contradicting or wrongly reinterpreting what Christ taught. An example of such issues is human sexuality, which

10. Cf. 2 Cor 4:16–18.
11. 1 Tim 6:6–10.
12. See Matt 6:27–33; Heb 13:5.
13. For an extended discussion of the challenges Islam poses to Christianity in Africa, see Akinade, "Islamic Challenges." In the same vein, O'Donovan (*Biblical Christianity*, 1) observes that while Africa has become the most Christian continent, Islam could become the dominant force in the continent's politics and government.

is confronting the worldwide church. At the heart of it is the view on one side that people of the same sex—both male or both female—could enter into a marital union with the blessing of the church and church-endorsed legal coverage. On the other side of the issue, the orthodoxy side, this view is of course ridiculous, contrary to the basic biblical teaching that God ordained marriage and that in God's design marriage is to be between one male adult and one female adult. This issue sent shock waves across the church worldwide and caused turbulences especially within the Anglican Communion, when in June 2003 the Rev. Gene Robinson, an openly gay priest, was elected and consecrated bishop of the Episcopal Diocese of New Hampshire in the USA.[14] The state of the debate aside, what is at issue is that such controversies imply a lack of spiritual maturity and constitute part of "every wind of doctrine," with the potential to uproot and ultimately destroy Christians who are not in a steady process of growing towards spiritual maturity.

Fifth, there are also numerous non-Christian and often anti-Christian religious thoughts and movements actively promoting different views of Christ, posing a significant threat to the spiritually immature Christian. For example, Islam with its resolve to make itself the religion of the world denies the divinity of Christ and would use a variety of strategies to lure the Christian to it and hence away from Christ. The notion that we all worship the same God is a deception not obvious to many, including Christians. Syncretism[15] may still be a significant issue against the Christian faith.

And sixth, the mass media, especially secular electronic media such as television, the Internet, videos and cinema, exert enormous influence on society. Although there are many ways in which the mass media are beneficial to society, there are many other ways in which the mass media are destructive to the society, the Christian community included. Often, for example, the content of the mass media is hostile to the Christian faith. The mass media is the biggest agent of popular culture,[16] the endless flow

---

14. Frank Griswold, Presiding Bishop of the Episcopal Church of the USA, supported and encouraged Robinson's election, in line with his position, which he declared when he took office, saying that the Episcopal Church was in conflict with Scripture and that the Holy Spirit was now leading the church to contradict the Bible (see Barnum, *Never Silent*, 242).

15. This is the tendency to fuse Christian truth with traditional religious beliefs, values, and practices, including ancestor worship, worship of lesser gods, and practices of witchcraft.

16. See Louw, *Media*; Hoover, *Mass Media Religion*.

of products, famous entertainers, live broadcasts of festivals or beauty contests, and many commercial advertisements. When people watch television, listen to the radio, or read the newspapers, they encounter popular culture. In that sense, the mass media create and disseminate "new" cultures, with its combination of various norms, moral principles, and values within the society. Often the mass media spread notions that all truth is relative, which in effect means there is no truth. The mass media also directs the public in specific issues and in that way produces public opinions regarding various important matters.

These realities present a significant force against the church and Christians. But also, as increasingly difficult as it is, this is the context within which the church has to carry out its witness as "the salt of the earth" and "the light of the world"[17] and continue to make disciples of all nations for Christ, as he commanded.[18] However, it should be noted that the importance of spiritual maturity for the church is much greater than these survival reasons for the church. It is simply the design and desire of Christ for his church.

It is therefore in order to make some recommendations:

First, spiritual maturity deserves to be a central part of biblical studies. If Christian spiritual maturity is the ultimate goal of the Christian life, and if the essence and life of the Christian faith are the primary focus of the New Testament, then spiritual maturity deserves a place of prominence in biblical studies, and its importance to the life and work of the church calls for renewed consideration of it as an important area of academic inquiry, particularly within New Testament studies.

Second, the church at large needs to be intentional and systematic in developing and implementing authentic programs to continue building the body of Christ. The leadership of the church in general needs itself to be in the process of striving towards full spiritual maturity. A church organized and administered by leaders who lack spiritual maturity can only be a church of largely spiritually immature members.

Third, spiritual maturity must form an important part of the modern-day Christian scholarship agenda. In a time of religious fundamentalism, even discussion of spiritual maturity may be viewed with disdain. It might appear as if the goal is to promote fundamentalism of another kind. This need not be the case. In fact, this is the more reason why Christian scholars

17. Matt 5:13–16.
18. Matt 28:19–20.

would want to bring the subject of spiritual maturity into their academic agenda. It is possible to have a theological perspective of spiritual maturity or, from a practical side, programs that would effectively contribute towards continued spiritual growth in the church in the various contexts of the church's witness in the world of the twenty-first century.

Fourth and finally, research is needed in the area of spiritual maturity for the church, to inform concerted efforts to continue building up Christians "Until we all attain the full measure of the stature of Christ."

Bibliography

Abbott, T. K. *A Critical and Exegetical Commentary on the Epistle to the Ephesians and to the Colossians.* International Critical Commentary. Edinburgh, Scotland: T. & T. Clark, 1968.

Akinade, A. E. "Islamic Challenges in African Christianity". In *African Christianity: An African Story*, edited by O. U. Kalu, 117–37. Pretoria: University of Pretoria, 2005.

Amador, J. D. H. *Academic Constraints in Rhetorical Criticism of the New Testament: An introduction to a Rhetoric of Power.* Sheffield, UK: Sheffield Academic Press, 1999.

Andrews, J. R. *The Practice of Rhetorical Criticism.* 2nd ed. New York & London: Longman, 1990.

Aristotle. *The Rhetoric of Aristotle.* Translated by Lane Cooper. Englewood Cliffs, NJ: Prentice-Hall, 1932.

Arnold, C. E. *Ephesians: Power and Magic. The Concept of Power in Ephesians in Light of Its Historical Setting.* Society for New Testament Studies Monograph Series 63. Cambridge, UK: Cambridge University Press, 1989.

Augustine, St. A. *On Christian Doctrine.* Translation of *De Doctrina Christiana*. Edited and translated by R. P. H. Green. Oxford Early Christian Texts. Oxford: Clarendon, 1995.

Aune, D. E. *The New Testament in Its Literary Environment.* Philadelphia: Westminster, 1987.

Babbie, E. *Survey Research Methods.* 2nd ed. Belmont, CA: Wadsworth, 1990.

Bailey, K. D. *Methods of Social Research.* 3rd ed. New York: Free Press, 1987.

Balch, D. L. "Household Codes." In *Greco-Roman Literature and the New Testament*, edited by D. E. Aune, 25–50. SBL Sources for Biblical Study 21. Atlanta, GA: Scholars Press, 1988.

Barnum, T. *Never Silent: How Third World Missionaries Are Now Bringing the Gospel to the US.* Colorado Springs, CO: Eleison, 2008.

Best, E. *A Critical and Exegetical Commentary on Ephesians.* International Critical Commentary. New York & London: T. & T. Clark, 1998.

Bitzer, L. F. "The Rhetorical Situation." In G. Campbell, *Philosophy and Rhetoric*, 1:1–14. Carbondale: Southern Illinois University Press, 1968.

———. "The Rhetorical Situation." In G. Campbell, *Philosophy and Rhetoric*, 1:1–24. Carbondale: Southern Illinois University Press, 1988.

Black, C. C. "Keeping Up with Recent Studies. Xvi. rhetorical Criticism and Biblical Interpretation." *The Expository Times* 100 (1989) 252–58.

Black, E. *Rhetorical Criticism: A Study in Method.* Madison: University of Wisconsin Press, 1965.

———. *Rhetorical Criticism: A Study in Method.* Madison: University of Wisconsin Press, 1978.

Bibliography

Black, M. *Models and Metaphors: Studies in Language and Philosophy*. New York: Cornell University Press, 1962.

Bloomquist, L. G. "The Role of the Audience in the Determination of the Argumentation: The Gospel of Luke and the Acts of the Apostles." In *Rhetorical Argumentation in Biblical Texts: Essays from the Lund 2000 Conference*, edited by A. Ericksson, T. H. Olbritch, and W. Ubelacker, 157–73. Harrisburg, PA: Trinity, 2002.

Boice, J. M. *Ephesians: An Expositional Commentary*. Grand Rapids: Baker, 1997.

Bormann, E. G. "Fantasy and Rhetorical Vision: The Rhetorical Criticism of Social Reality." *Quarterly Journal of Speech* 58 (December 1972) 396–407.

———. "Fantasy and Rhetorical Vision: Ten Years Later." *Quarterly Journal of Speech* 68 (August 1982) 288–305.

———. *The Force of Fantasy: Restoring the American Dream*. Carbondale, IL: Southern Illinois University Press, 2001.

———. "Symbolic Convergence Theory: A Communication Formulation." *Journal of Communication* 35 (Autumn 1985) 128–38.

Brembeck, W. L., and W. S. Howell. *Persuasion: A Means of Social Influence*. 2nd ed. Englewood Cliffs, NJ: Prentice-Hall, 1976.

Brinton, A. "Situation in the Theory of Rhetoric." *Philosophy and Rhetoric* 14 (1981) 234–48.

Briscoe, D. S. *Let's Get Moving: A Bible Commentary for Laymen*. Glendale, CA: Regal, 1978.

Brown, D. *The Da Vinci Code*. London: Corgis, 2004.

Burke, K. *A Rhetoric of Motives*. Berkeley, CA: University of California Press, 1969.

Cameron, A. *Christianity and the Rhetoric of Empire: The Development of Christian Discourse*. Berkeley: University of California Press, 1991.

Campbell, K. K. "The Forum: Conventional Wisdom-Traditional Form: A Rejoinder." *Quarterly Journal of Speech* 58 (1972) 454.

Cicero. *De Oratore*. Vols. 1 & 2. Loeb Classical Library. London: Heinemann, 1948.

Classen, C. J. *Rhetorical Criticism of the New Testament*. Boston: Brill, 2002.

Conley, T. M.. *Rhetoric in the European Tradition*. New York & London: Longman, 1990.

Corley, B. "A Student's Primer for Exegesis." In *Biblical hermeneutics: A Comprehensive Introduction to Interpreting Scripture*, edited by B. Corley, S. Lemke, and G. Lovejoy, 1–19. Nashville: Broadman & Holman, 1996.

Cornelius, E. M. "The Effectiveness of 1Thessalonians: A Rhetorical-Critical Study." D. Phil. thesis, University of Stellenbosch, 1998.

Creswell, J. W. *Research Design: Qualitative and Quantitative Approaches*. Thousand Oaks, CA: Sage, 1994.

Croft, A. J. "The Functions of Rhetorical Criticism." In *The Province of Rhetoric*, edited by J. Schwartz and J. A. Rycenga, 403–14. New York: Ronald Press, 1965.

Cronkhite, G. *Persuasion: Speech and Behavioural Change*. Indianapolis: Bobbs-Merrill, 1969.

Cullmann, O. *Salvation History*. 2nd ed. London: SCM, 1967.

De Klerk, B. J., and F. J. van Rensburg. *Making a Sermon: A Guide for Reformed Exegesis and Preaching: Applied to 1 Peter 2:11-12, 18-25*. Potchefstroom: Potchefstroom Theological, 2005.

Dulle, J. A. "Technical Commentary on Ephesians 4:7–16." Online: http://www.apostolic.net/biblicalstudies/ephesians4716.htm.

Bibliography

Edwards, M. J., editor. *Galatians, Ephesians, Philippians*. Ancient Christian Commentary on Scripture, New Testament 8. Downers Groove, IL: InterVarsity, 1999.
Elliott, J. H. *A Home for the Homeless: A Social-Scientific Criticism of 1 Peter, Its Situation and Strategy*. Minneapolis: Fortress, 1990.
"Measure." *Encyclopaedia Britannica*. Vol. 15. Chicago: Encyclopaedia Britannica, 1971.
Encyclopaedia Britannica. Vol. 9. Chicago: Encyclopaedia Britannica, 1965.
Ericksson, A. "Contrary Arguments in Paul's Letters." In *Rhetorical Criticism and the Bible*, edited by S. E. Porter and D. L. Stamps, 336–54. Journal of New Testament Studies Series 195. Sheffield, UK: Sheffield Academic Press, 2002.
Fee, G. D., and D. Stuart. *How to Read the Bible for Its Worth: A Guide to Understanding the Bible*. London: Scripture Union, 1982.
———. *How to Read the Bible for Its Worth: A Guide to Understanding the Bible*. 3rd ed. Grand Rapids: Zondervan, 2003.
Fink, A., and J. Kosecoff. *How to Conduct Surveys: A Step-by-Step Guide*. Newbury Park, CA: Sage, 1985.
Foss, S. K. *Rhetorical Criticism: Explorations and Practice*. Illinois: Waveland, 1989.
Foulkes, F. *Ephesians*. Rev. ed. Tyndale New Testament Commentaries. Leicester, UK: InterVarsity, 1989.
Fowler, F. J. *Survey Research Methods*. Newbury Park, CA: Sage, 1988.
Garlow, J. L. *The Da Vince Code Breaker: An Easy-to-Use Fact Checker*. Minneapolis: Bethany House, 2006.
Goodspeed, E. J. *The Meaning of Ephesians*. Chicago: University of Chicago Press, 1933.
Grudem, W. *Systematic Theology: An Introduction to Biblical Doctrine*. Leicester, UK: InterVarsity, 1994.
Gumede, M. W. E. "Keeping the Unity of the Holy Spirit: An Exegetical and Pastoral Study of Ephesians 4:3." Unpublished MA diss., Potchefstroomse Universiteit vir Christelike Hoër Onderwys, 2000.
Guthrie, D. *The Pauline Epistles: New Testament Introduction*. London: Tyndale, 1961.
Hasel, G. *New Testament Theology: Basic Issues in the Current Debate*. Grand Rapids: Eerdmans, 1978.
Hayes, J. H., editor. *Old Testament Form Criticism*. San Antonio: Trinity University Press, 1974.
Heil, J. P. *Ephesians: Empowerment to Walk in Love for the Unity of All in Christ*. Studies in Biblical Literature 13. Atlanta: Society of Biblical Literature, 2007.
Hellholm, D. "Enthymematic Argumentation in Paul: The Case of Romans 6." In *Paul in His Hellenistic Context*, edted by T. Engberg-Pedersen, 119–79. Minneapolis: Fortress, 1995.
Hendriksen, W. *Ephesians*. New Testament Commentary. Edinburgh, UK: Banner of Truth, 1967.
Hill, F. I. "Aristotle's Rhetorical Theory: With a Synopsis of Aristotle's Rhetoric." In *A Synoptic History of Classical Rhetoric*, edited by J. J. Murphy and R. A. Katula, 51–109. 2nd ed. Davis, CA: Hermagoras, 1995.
Hodge, C. *A Commentary on the Epistle to the Ephesians*. London, UK: The Burner of Truth Trust. 1964.
Hodge, C. *Ephesians*. Crossway Classic Commentaries. Wheaton, IL: Crossway, 1994.
Holland, G. "Paul's Use of Irony as a Rhetorical Technique." In *The rhetorical Analysis of Scripture: Essays from the 1995 London Conference*, edited by S. E. Porter and T.

Bibliography

H. Olbrechts, 234–248. Journal of New Testament Supplement Series 146. Sheffield, UK: Sheffield Academic, 1997.

Hoover, S. M. *Mass Media Religion: The Social Sources of the Electronic Church*. London: Sage, 1988.

Hughes, F. W. *Early Christian Rhetoric and 2 Thessalonians*. Journal for the study of the New Testament, Supplement Series 30. Sheffield: Sheffield Academic, 1989.

Janse Van Rensburg, Fika. "The Analysis of Syntactic Structure in the Greek New Testament: The Draft of a Method, Illustrated with Romans 8." Th.D. thesis, Potchefstroom University, 1981.

Jasper, D. "Reflections on the London Conference on the Rhetorical Analysis of Scripture." In *The Rhetorical analysis of Scripture: Essays from the 1995 London Conference*, edited by S. E. Porter and T. H. Olbrechts, 476–82. Journal for the Study of the New Testament, Supplement Series 146. Sheffield: Sheffield Academic, 1997.

Jeal, R. R. "Rhetorical Argumentation in the Letter to the Ephesians." In *Rhetorical Argumentation in Biblical Texts: Essays from the Lund 2000 Conference*, edited by A. Ericksson, T. H. Olbritch, and W. Ubelacke, 310–24. Harrisburg, PA: Trinity, 2002.

Johanson, B. C. *To All the Brethren: A Text-Linguistic and Rhetorical Approach to 1 Thessalonians*. Coniectanea Biblica New Testament Series 16. Stockholm: Almqvist & Wiksell, 1987.

Kaiser, W. C. *Toward an Exegetical Theology: Biblical Exegesis for Preaching and Teaching*. Grand Rapids: Baker, 1981.

Kennedy, D. J. *The Da Vinci Myth versus the Gospel Truth*. Wheaton, IL: Crossway, 2006.

Kennedy, G. A. *Classical Rhetoric and Its Christian and Secular Tradition from Ancient and Modern Times*. Chapel Hill: University of North Carolina Press, 1980.

———. *New Testament Interpretation through Rhetorical Criticism*. Chapel Hill: University of North Carolina Press, 1984.

Kern, P. H. *Rhetoric and Galatians: Assessing an Approach to Paul's Epistle*. Society for New Testament Studies, Monograph Series 101. Cambridge, UK: Cambridge University Press, 1998.

Kessler, M. "A Methodological Setting for Rhetorical Criticism." *Semitics* 4 (1974) 22–36.

Kirby, J. L. *Ephesians, Baptism and Pentecost*. Montreal: McGill University Press, 1968.

Kitchen, M. *Ephesians*. New York: Routledge, 1994.

Kittredge, C. B. *Community and Authority: The Rhetoric of Obedience in the Pauline Tradition*. Harrisburg, PA: Trinity, 1998.

Klein, W. W., C. L. Blomberg, and R. L. Hubbard. *Introduction to Biblical Interpretation*. Dallas: Word, 1993.

———. *Introduction to Biblical Interpretation*. Rev. ed. Nashville: T. Nelson, 2004.

Ladd, G. E. *A Theology of the New Testament*. Grand Rapids: Zondervan, 1974.

Leedy, P.D. *Practical Research: Planning and Design*. 3rd ed. New York: Macmillan, 1985.

Leff, M. "Topical Invention and Metaphoric Interaction." *Southern Speech Communication Journal* 48 (Spring 1983) 214–29.

Lemmer, R. "Rhetoric and Metaphor, and the Metaphysical in the Letter to the Ephesians." In *Rhetorical Criticism and the Bible*, edited by S. E. Porter and D. L. Stamps, 458–80. Journal for the Study of the New Testament, Supplement Series 195. Sheffield, UK: Sheffield Academic, 2002.

Levison, J. R. "Did the Spirit Inspire Rhetoric?: An Exploration of George Kennedy's Definition of Early Christian Rhetoric." In *Persuasive Artistry: Studies in New Testament Rhetoric in Honour of George A. Kennedy*, edited by D. F. Watson, 25–40.

Bibliography

Journal for the Study of the New Testament, Supplement Series 50. Sheffield, UK: Sheffield Academic, 1991

Liefield, W. L. *Ephesians*. IVP New Testament Commentary Series. Downers Grove, IL: InterVarsity. 1997.

Lincoln, A. *Ephesians*. Word Biblical Commentary 42. Dallas: Word, 1990.

Lloyd-Jones, D. M. *Christian Unity: An Exposition of Ephesians 4:1–16*. Grand Rapids: Baker, 1980.

Longman, T., III. *Literary Approaches to Biblical Interpretation*. Foundations of Contemporary Interpretation 3. Grand Rapids: Zondervan, 1987.

Louw, P. E. *The Media and Cultural Production*. London, UK: Sage, 2001.

Lutzer, E. W. *The Da Vinci Deception*. Vereeniging, SA: Christian Art Publishers, 2005.

MacArthur, J. *Twelve Ordinary Men: How the Master Shaped His Disciples for Greatness and What He Wants to Do with You*. Nashville: T. Nelson, 2002.

MacArthur, J. F. *Ephesians*. MacArthur New Testament commentary series. Chicago: Moody Press, 1986.

Mack, B. L. *Rhetoric and the New Testament*. Minneapolis: Fortress, 1990.

Malherbe, A. J. *Moral Exhortation: A Greco-Roman Sourcebook*. Library of Early Christianity. Philadelphia: Westminster, 1986.

———. *Social Aspects of early Christianity*. 2nd ed. Philadelphia: Fortress, 1983.

Marshall, I. H. "Introduction." In *New Testament Interpretation: Essays on Principles and Methods*, edited by I. H. Marshall. Grand Rapids: Eerdmans, 1991.

Martin, R. P. "An Epistle in Search of a Life-Setting." *Expository Times* 79 (1968) 296–302.

———. *Ephesians, Colossians and Philemon: A Bible Commentary for Teaching and Preaching*. Atlanta: John Knox, 1991.

Mbennah, E. D. "Communication and Social Change in Southern Africa: Foundations, Issues and Strategies." In *Sustainable Social Development: Critical Issues*, edited by H. C. Marais, V. Muthien, N. S. Janse van Rensburg, M. P. Maaga, G. F. De Wet, and C. J. Coetzee, 83–96. Menlo Park, South Africa: Network, 2001.

———. "The Impact of Audience World View on Speaker Credibility in Persuasive Speaking: The Case of Afrocentric and Eurocentric Audiences." Unpublished Ph.D. thesis, Potchefstroomse Universiteit vir Christelike Hoër Onderwys, 1999.

McCown, W., and J. E. Massey. *Interpreting God's Word for Today: An Inquiry into Hermeneutics from a Biblical Theological Perspective*. Indianapolis: Anderson Warner, 1982.

Meynet, R. *Rhetorical Analysis: An Introduction to Biblical Rhetoric*. Journal of the Society of Old Testament Studies 256. Sheffield, UK: Sheffield Academic, 1998.

Miller, G. R. "On Being Persuaded: Some Basic Distinctions." In *Persuasion: New Directions in Theory and Research*, edited by M. E. Roloff and G. R. Miller, 1–28. Beverly Hills, CA: Sage, 1980.

Muddiman, J. *A Commentary on the Epistle to the Ephesians*. Black's New Testament Commentaries. London & New York: Continuum, 2001.

Muilenburg, J. 1969. "Form Criticism and Beyond." *Journal of Biblical Literature* 88 (2001) 1–18.

Newell, R. "Questionnaires." In *Researching Social Life*, edited by N. Gilbert, 94–115. London: Sage, 1996.

Norusis, M. *The SPSS Guide to Data Analysis for SPSS/PC+*. Chicago: SPSS, 1988.

———. *The SPSS/PC+ Advanced Statistics 4.0*. Chicago: SPSS, 1991.

Bibliography

O'Brien, P. *The Epistle to the Ephesians*. Pillar New Testament Commentary. Grand Rapids: Eerdmans, 1999.

O'Donovan, W. *Biblical Christianity in Modern Africa*. Cumbria, UK: Paternoster, 2000.

Pattie, D. *The Religious Dimensions of biblical Texts*. Atlanta: Scholars, 1990.

Perelman, C., and L. Olbrechts-Tyteca. *The New Rhetoric: A Treatise on Argumentation*. Notre Dame: University of Notre Dame Press, 1969.

———. *The New Rhetoric and the Humanities: Essays in Rhetoric and Its Applications*. Boston: D. Reidel, 1979.

Perry, S. "Rhetorical functions of the infestation metaphor in Hitler's rhetoric." *Central states speech journal*, 34: 229–235. Winter. 1983.

Pirouet, M. L. *Black Evangelists: The spread of Christianity in Uganda 1891–1914*. London, UK: Rex Collings. 1978.

Pogoloff, S. M. "Isocrates and Contemporary Hermeneutics." In *Persuasive artistry: Studies in New Testament Rhetoric in Honour of George A. Kennedy*, edited by D. F. Watson, 338–62. Journal for the Study of the New Testament, Supplement Series 50. Sheffield, UK: Sheffield Academic, 1991.

Porter, S. E. "Ancient Rhetorical Analysis and Discourse Analysis of the Pauline Corpus." In *The Rhetorical Analysis of Scripture: Essays from the 1995 London Conference*, edited by S. E. Porter and T. H. Olbrechts, 249–274. Journal of the Study of the New Testament, Supplement Series 146. Sheffield, UK: Sheffield Academic, 1997.

Porter, S. E., and D. L. Stamps, editors. *Rhetorical Criticism and the Bible*. Journal of the Study of the New Testament, Supplement Series 195. Sheffield, UK: Sheffield Academic, 2002.

Poythress, V. S. *Science and Hermeneutics: Implications of Scientific Method for Biblical Interpretation*. Foundations of Contemporary Interpretation 6. Grand Rapids: Academie, 1988.

Prince, G. *Narratology: The Form and Functioning of Narrative*. New York: Mouton, 1982.

Procter, M. "Analysing Survey Data." In *Researching Social Life*, edited by N. Gilbert, 239–54. London: Sage, 1996.

Richards, E. R. *Paul and First-Century Letter Writing: Secretaries, Composition and Collection*. Downers Grove, IL: InterVarsity, 2004.

Richards, I. A. *The Philosophy of Rhetoric*. London: Oxford University Press, 1936.

Robbins, V. K. "Argumentative Textures in Socio-Rhetorical Interpretation." In *Rhetorical Argumentation in Biblical Texts: Essays from the Lund 2000 Conference*, edited by A. Ericksson, T. H. Olbritch, and W. Ubelacker, 27–65. Harrisburg, PA: Trinity, 2002.

———. *Jesus the Teacher: A Socio-Rhetorical Interpretation of Mark*. New York: Fortress, 1984.

———. "The Present and Future of Rhetorical Analysis." In *The Rhetorical Analysis of Scripture: Essays from the 1995 London Conference*, edited by S. E. Porter and T. H. Olbrechts, 24–49. Journal of the Study of the New Testament, Supplement Series 146. Sheffield, UK: Sheffield Academic, 1997.

———. "Rhetorical Analysis of Biblical Documents in the Past Decade with Special Focus on the Seven 'Pepperdine' Conferences." Emory University and University of Stellenbosch. Paper presented at the Heidelberg Rhetoric Conference, July 25, 2002. Online: http://www.ars-rhetorica.net/Queen/VolumeSpecialIssue2/Articles/Robbins.pdf.

Robinson, J. A. *St. Paul's Epistle to the Ephesians. A Revised Text and Translation with Exposition and Notes*. London J. Clarke, 1971.

Bibliography

Roetzel, C. J. *The World that Shaped the New Testament*. London: SCM, 1985.

Scheidel, T. M. *Persuasive Speaking*. Glenview, IL: Scott, Foresman, 1967.

Schnackenburg, R. *The Epistle to the Ephesians*. Translated by H. Heron. Edinburgh, Scotland: T. & T. Clark, 1991.

Schüssler Fiorenza, E. *The Book of Revelation: Justice and Judgment*. Philadelphia: Fortress, 1984.

———. "Challenging the rhetorical half-turn: Feminist and rhetorical biblical criticism." In *Rhetoric and Ethic: The Politics of Biblical Studies*, edited by S. E. Porter and T. H. Olbrechts, 83–102. Minneapolis: Fortress, 1999.

———. "The Ethics of Interpretation: De-Centering Biblical Scholarship." *Journal of Biblical Literature* 107 (1988) 3–17.

Scott, R. L., and B. L. Brock. *Methods of Rhetorical Criticism*. New York: Harper & Row, 1972.

Shoemaker, P. J., and M. E. McCombs. "Survey Research." In *Research methods in mass communication*, edited by G. H. Stemple III and B. H. Westley, 150–72. 2nd ed. Englewood Cliffs, NJ: Prentice Hall, 1986.

Simons, H. W. *Persuasion: Understanding, Practice, and Analysis*. 2nd ed. New York: Random House, 1986.

Simpson, E. K., and F. F. Bruce. *The Epistles of Ephesians and Colossians*. New International Commentary on the New Testament. Grand Rapids: Eerdmans, 1957.

Stott, J. R. W. *The Message of Ephesians: God's New Society*. The Bible Speaks Today. Leicester, UK: InterVarsity, 1979.

Stowers, S. E. *A Reading of Romans: Justice, Jews and the Gentiles*. New Haven, CT: Yale University Press, 1994.

Stowers, S. K. *Letter Writing in Greco-Roman Antiquity: Library of Early Christianity*. Philadelphia: Westminster, 1986.

———. "Social Typification and the Classification of Ancient letters." In *The Social World of Formative Christianity and Judaism: Essays in Tribute to Howard Clark Lee*, edited by J. Neusner, P. Borgen, E. Frerichs, and R. Horsely, 78–90. Philadelphia: Fortress, 1988.

Suleiman, S. R. "Introduction: Varieties of Audience-Oriented Criticism". In *The Reader in the Text: Essays on Audience and Interpretation*, edited by S. R. Suleiman and L. I. Crosman, 2–45. Princeton, NJ: Princeton University Press, 1980.

Sullivan, D. L., and C. Anibile. "The Epideictic Dimension of Galatians as Formative Rhetoric: The Inscription of Early Christian Community." *Rhetorica* 18/2 (2000) 117–45.

Thiessen, H. C. *Lectures in Systematic Theology*. Rev. by Vernon D. Doerksen. Grand Rapids: Eerdmans, 1979.

Thompson, J. "Hermeneutic inquiry". In *Advancing Nursing Science through Research*, edited by L. Moody, 2:223–80. Newbury Park, NY: Sage, 1990.

Thonssen, L., A. C. Baird, and W. W. Braden. *Speech Criticism*. 2nd ed. New York: Ronald Press, 1970.

Trible, P. *Rhetorical Criticism: Context, Method and the Book of Jonah*. Guides of Biblical Scholarship. Minneapolis: Fortress, 1994.

Trochim, W. M. K. *The Research Methods Knowledge Base*. 2nd ed. Cincinnati: Atomic, 2001.

Virkler, H. A. *Hermeneutics: Principles and Processes of Biblical Interpretation*. Grand Rapids: Baker, 1981.

Bibliography

Vorster, J. N. "Why Opt for a Rhetorical Approach?" *Noetestamentica* 29/2 (1995) 393–418.

White, J. L. "Ancient Greek Letters." In *Greco-Roman literature and the New Testament*, edited by D. E. Aune, 85–105. SBL Sources for Biblical Study 21. Atlanta, GA: Scholars, 1988.

Wichelns, H. A. "The Literary Criticism of Oratory." In *Methods of Rhetorical Criticism: A Twentieth-Century Perspective*, edited by B. L. Brock, and R. L. Scott. 2nd ed. Detroit: Wayne State University Press, 1980.

Wilson, D. J. "Back to Conversation." In *Back to Basics: Rediscovering the richness of the Reformed Faith*, edited by D. G. Hagopian, 6–64. Phillipsburg, NJ: P&R, 1996.

Wolvaardt, B. *How to Interpret the Bible: A Do-It-Yourself Manual*. Harpenden, Hertfordshire, UK: Veritas College, 1999.

Wuellner, W. "Rhetoric Criticism." In *The Postmodern Bible*, edited by E. A. Castelli, S. D. Moore, G. A. Phillips, and R. M. Schwartz, 149–86. New Haven, CT: Yale University, 1995.

———. "Where Is Rhetorical Criticism Taking Us?" *Catholic Bible Quarterly* 49 (1987) 448–63.

www.ingramcontent.com/pod-product-compliance
Lightning Source LLC
Chambersburg PA
CBHW070943160426

43193CB00011B/1792